Sexuality Education
Across Cultures

· ·

Janice M. Irvine

· ·

Sexuality Education Across Cultures

Working With Differences

Jossey-Bass Publishers
San Francisco

Substantial discounts on bulk quantities of Jossey-Bass books are available to corporations, professional associations, and other organizations. For details and discount information, contact the special sales department at Jossey-Bass Inc., Publishers. (415) 433–1740; Fax (800) 605–2665.

For sales outside the United States, please contact your local Paramount Publishing International Office.

 Manufactured in the United States of America on Lyons Falls Pathfinder Tradebook. This paper is acid-free and 100 percent totally chlorine-free.

Library of Congress Cataloging-in-Publication Data

Irvine, Janice M.
    Sexuality education across cultures / Janice M. Irvine.
        p. cm. — (Jossey-Bass social and behavorial science series) (The Jossey-Bass health series)
    Includes bibliographical references and index.
    ISBN 0-7879-0154-7 (alk. paper)
    1. Sex instruction. 2. Multiculturalism. 3. Multicultural education. I. Title.
    II. Series.
    HQ56.3.I78   1995
    306.7—dc20   95-18042

HB Printing   10 9 8 7 6 5 4 3 2 1   FIRST EDITION

A joint publication in
The Jossey-Bass Social and Behavioral Science Series
and
The Jossey-Bass Health Series

To Ellen Keniston

Contents

Preface

For those of us who teach about sexuality it is, it seems, the best of times and the worst of times. We are enjoying unprecedented success in a time of deep cultural anxiety about sexuality.

On the one hand, there is much to celebrate. More and more people recognize the need for sexuality education, in part because of heightened national attention to teenage pregnancy and AIDS. In public opinion polls, most parents claim to support sexuality education in the public schools. More states than ever before require sexuality education in the public schools.[1] And many professional schools train doctors, nurses, psychologists, and social workers to discuss sexuality with their patients and clients. We can feel justifiably proud of such mainstream acceptance, for these gains have not been easily won.

On the other hand, talking about sexuality may still be discomfiting at best and dangerous at worst. United States Surgeon General Joycelyn Elders was fired in late 1994 for even suggesting that children should perhaps be taught about masturbation in sexuality education courses. Sexuality education remains one of the most embattled fields of instruction. Controversies over teaching about sexuality in the public schools have increased since 1990, with school board and community meetings sometimes erupting in shouting matches over what should be taught. Many people are still most comfortable when sexuality remains invisible.

It is no surprise that those of us whose job it is to teach about sexuality, whether we are educators, parents, or health professionals, can feel caught in this cultural tension between sexual literacy and sexual silence. There is much to be anxious about in such an ambivalent climate. Many teachers feel that they are simply doing the best they can in the face of too little money, too little time, and too many attacks on their achievements. Some of them didn't want to teach sexuality classes to begin with, but as nurses, coaches, or home economics teachers they were drafted into service by budget-conscious administrators. Parents can feel uninformed and unprepared to discuss sexual topics with their children. Professionals worry about being intrusive by discussing clients' sexual health. And yet all these concerns are tempered by the recognition that it has never been more important to talk about sexuality.

The urgency that many of us feel to teach about sexual risks, sexual health, and sexual pleasure prompts an ongoing reevaluation of our methods, as we continually search for better ways to communicate about sexuality. How, we wonder, can we fashion the most effective programs? How can we reach as many people as possible? What are the best ways to frame our messages? Are we speaking in ways that can really be heard?

In order to answer these questions we must consider our audiences, which leads inevitably to a recognition that the individuals in them are often from very different backgrounds. As most educators know, our audiences and classrooms are becoming more culturally diverse. By the year 2000, students of color will comprise approximately 46 percent of school-age youth in the United States.[2] The differences among people, the way that these differences shape their sexual cultures, and the implications of cultural diversity for teaching about sexuality form the central focus of this book.

Currently, as educational researchers Janie Ward and Jill Taylor point out, most sexuality education in the U.S. reflects a white, middle-class, heterosexual male bias.[3] This is not surprising and is not a criticism unique to sexuality education. All educational pro-

grams in our society share that bias, and this has motivated the contemporary movement for multicultural education. We know that
programs that fail to recognize cultural diversity are susceptible to
a variety of "breakdowns" in which misunderstandings are likely to
occur across lines of ethnic or other difference.[4]

When we teach about sexuality, such breakdowns might result
from using a language in which sexual meanings are shared by a
white, middle-class audience but are unfamiliar to or inappropriate
for other groups. Or they might come from assuming that certain
sexual behaviors are favored by everyone instead of recognizing that
cultures assign different values to sexual practices. Breakdowns in
sexual communication are likely whenever the speaker assumes that
any aspect of sexuality is universally shared.

This book examines cultural differences and sexuality. It is based
on my experiences as a sociologist who teaches college courses on
sexuality, culture, and identity and as a community sexuality educator with over twenty years of experience working with such organizations as schools, agencies, and parent groups. Since the mid
1980s, I have seen in both the academy and the community a growing recognition of the need to challenge cultural bias in education
and to fully address diversity. Yet there is widespread disagreement
and confusion over how best to achieve multiculturalism.

Over the years, I have participated in countless efforts to
achieve diversity in organizations, programs, and curricula. Some
of the earlier approaches were simplistic, such as efforts to insert
photographs of people of color into texts and brochures without
altering the basic point of view. The multicultural panel (which I
discuss more fully in Chapter Two), in which speakers of different
racial and ethnic backgrounds professed to speak for entire communities ("black people think like this," "Latinos behave like
that"), was likewise ineffective. There were also complicated hiring decisions within predominantly European-American organizations in which the impossible dream was to find the individual who
was so perfectly multicultural as to be effective in all communities

of color. These were weak attempts motivated, in most cases, by the best intentions.

As time has passed we have grown more knowledgeable and sophisticated about how to achieve a multiculturalism that is truly transformative rather than simply window dressing. It is still a complicated and challenging task, especially in a society in which multicultural education has come under almost as much attack by critics as sexuality education. Widespread social discrimination on the basis of race and ethnicity, gender, sexual identity, and other differences can serve as a roadblock for the most finely crafted educational programs. Nevertheless, I have been a part of highly effective multicultural efforts, and this book has been shaped by what I have learned from both the successes and the failures.

Three interrelated beliefs form the foundation of *Sexuality Education Across Cultures*. First, there is no simple blueprint for developing effective multicultural sexuality education. Unfortunately, I am not able to describe what does work in as clear and straightforward a fashion as what doesn't work. This may be disappointing for some, but it will not be a surprise to most educators who know that effective programming rarely follows a formula. Instead, it is the result of a complex mix of knowledge, awareness, and skills.

Second, those who teach about sexuality are themselves the most important resource for working effectively with cultural difference. We are called upon to communicate interculturally all the time. Even if we are teaching a group with which we share a racial identity, there will likely be other differences—of, say, ethnicity, gender, or socioeconomic class—among audience members. All of these factors can shape sexual beliefs, values, and behaviors in different ways. No one, including sexuality educators, can become expert in the sex/gender systems of every culture. But through a deepened awareness of our own sexual culture, and a commitment to learning about some other cultures, educators can develop the skills for working with difference.

Finally, an essential tool for effective multicultural sexuality education is knowledge of how sexuality and culture each operate and how they interact. There have been important advances in the last several years in how we understand these concepts. For example, we have increasing evidence that challenges the popular idea that sexuality is largely shaped by our biological drives. Newer scholarship shows how sexuality is an aspect of social life that is created, defined, and regulated differently by various cultural groups. Similarly, the meaning of culture—and especially our ideas about race—has been a topic of debate.

This book will help sexuality educators become familiar with the current debates about culture and sexuality. It is unique in several ways. As of this writing, it is the only book to assist those who teach about sexuality in the important task of addressing cultural differences. Just as significant, however, is its goal of bringing into schools and communities a set of insights and topics to be debated that have usually been confined to the academy. Based on my community experience, I am convinced that an understanding of current theory and research on sexuality and culture can make a profound difference in crafting effective programs.

My approach in this book is to first present theoretical views of sexuality and culture and then in later chapters show how these theories operate. Chapter One focuses on two views of sexuality: essentialism and social constructionism. I will show that even though most sexuality education is based on essentialist ideas there is compelling evidence that sexuality is better understood as a creation of our social worlds. Social construction theory, I argue, is an important tool for understanding cultural diversity in sexuality. Chapter Two takes up the important issue of defining culture, for our ideas about culture and how it works are crucial in program development. We will look at the intersection of culture and sexuality through scripting theory, which offers us a useful way of analyzing how culture shapes our sexual thoughts, feelings, and behaviors.

Sexuality educators work in a historical context, and the events and belief systems that have preceded us have an impact on our work. Therefore, it is important to understand how ideas about cultural difference and sexuality have historically been used to justify the marginalization of, and discrimination against, certain groups. Chapter Three looks at contemporary debates about the social construction of race and also includes a historical overview of racial and sexual stereotypes. In Chapter Four we examine how individuals from different cultures may differ in their ways of being sexual and establishing sexual identities. There is discussion of such topics as teenage pregnancy, masturbation, oral sex, anal sex, and the identity categories of heterosexuality and homosexuality. In Chapter Five I argue that gender and sexuality interact in complicated ways. When we add cultural differences into this mix, we see that an individual's sexual worldview can be profoundly shaped by particular cultural beliefs about what it means to be a man or a woman.

Chapter Six targets the important question of cultural differences in sexual communication. I will argue that an understanding of diverse perspectives on sexual speech is crucial for sexuality educators. Risk is the topic of Chapter Seven. I will argue that, like sexuality, risk is an arena of social life whose meanings can differ by culture. We will see how ideas about both risk and sexuality are shaped by a number of factors, including families. Finally, the challenge of becoming interculturally competent is discussed in the Epilogue. All of us, with awareness of our own culture's and others' sex/gender systems, can communicate across cultures.

Sexuality Education Across Cultures is not a prescription for a curriculum. Rather, it is a sourcebook of information and research to help educators design a variety of curricula that will meet their specific educational needs. In each chapter I provide examples of problems that may face sexuality educators as they develop culturally appropriate programs.

There are two final points of which readers should be aware. First, although for simplicity I use the term *sexuality educator* throughout this book, I mean it in its broadest definition. Many professionals are in the position of communicating about sexual issues. They include social workers, psychologists, community organizers, nurses and physicians, health educators, college professors and staff, and teachers of all subjects. Parents are another group who, at one time or another, become sexuality educators. This book is addressed to all those who have the occasion to talk about sexuality with others.

Acknowledgments

The writing of *Sexuality Education Across Cultures* was prompted by the enthusiastic reception received for these ideas as I have presented them in training sessions and workshops over the last several years. I would like to thank the many participants for their encouragement. Sharon Thompson, Louise Rice, and Carolyn Stack gave me careful and insightful responses to early drafts; their comments have helped me to clarify and greatly improve my work. I am grateful for the assistance of Becky McGovern and Barbara Hill at Jossey-Bass and for reviewers' helpful comments. Thanks in particular to Carolyn Stack for her wit, intelligence, and support, all of which made this a better book.

Princeton, Massachusetts   Janice M. Irvine
June 1995

The Author

Janice M. Irvine is an assistant professor of sociology at the University of Massachusetts at Amherst. She received her B.A. degree (1973) and M.Ed. degree (1975) from Pennsylvania State University, both her M.A. degree (1981) and Ph.D. (1984) in sociology from Brandeis University, and her M.P.H. degree (1993) from Boston University. Before joining the faculty at the University of Massachusetts, she taught for five years at Tufts University.

Irvine's main area of research is the study of sexuality. She is the author of *Disorders of Desire: Sex and Gender in Modern American Sexology* (1990) and the editor of *Sexual Cultures and the Construction of Adolescent Identities* (1994). Her current research project, for which she received a Rockefeller Fellowship, is an examination of sexuality education controversies. She has worked, as both staff member and consultant, for a range of community-based organizations for over twenty years.

Sexuality Education
Across Cultures

Rethinking Sexuality

Our ideas about sexuality—what it is and where it comes from—
are critically important to sexuality education. That is because
how we think about sexuality shapes how we talk about it. Our ideas
and theories guide us in our work, whether it is designing a curriculum, brochure, workshop, or research project. Even if we are not
consciously aware of our assumptions about sexuality, they exert a
tremendous influence.

As we move toward our goal of effective multicultural sexuality
education, our success at designing culturally diverse programs begins
at this first stage of ideas. Some beliefs and assumptions about sexuality keep us narrowly focused on the individual while others encourage us to examine the role that different cultures play in making us
sexual people. In this chapter, I review the ongoing discussion, and
sometimes volatile debate, about two different theoretical perspectives on sexuality: essentialism and social construction theory. For
the most part, sexuality educators have been outside, and even
unaware of, these debates. Yet we have a high stake in them, for the
core assumptions of each perspective lead us to ask different questions about sexuality and result in different educational strategies.

In this chapter, I will describe in detail the central points of both
essentialism and social construction theory. My emphasis is on the
implications of each perspective for the ways that we approach particular dilemmas and challenges in sexuality education. As I discuss

below, most sexuality education is based on an essentialist view. But I strongly believe it is time to reevaluate the essentialist assumption in light of the exciting research revealing that our social worlds have a greater impact on our sexuality than does our biological makeup.

The Essentialist Assumption

To many in the United States, the word *sex* has a simple and narrow meaning: sexual intercourse. Most people don't ask for clarification when a friend talks about "having sex." They assume, and usually rightly so, that they know what she or he means. "Sex" might be exciting, forbidden, daring, or immoral, but it still usually refers to events that are primarily heterosexual and genital.

This assumption is slowly changing. Over the last two decades, educators have promoted a more comprehensive approach. We encourage a view of sex not just as the capacity for certain physical acts but as an aspect of an individual's total personality. As well as a physical dimension, sexuality includes emotions, beliefs, attitudes, and values.

This broader definition has been important for teachers and other health and human service professionals since it means that sexuality is not a small and isolated aspect of one's life but is woven through all aspects of who we are. It is now increasingly obvious to us that when we educate about pregnancy prevention or safer sex we must consider far more than teaching individuals the mechanics of behavior change. We know that individual decisions about sexual activity are related not just to knowledge about options but to such other factors as self-esteem and personal empowerment.

The idea persists, however, that sexuality lies exclusively in the realm of the individual. Even in this new, expanded definition of sexuality as an aspect of the total personality rather than simply genital activities, the emphasis remains on sexuality as a deep and natural individual expression. This perspective is called *essentialism*, and it is the most common way of thinking about sexuality in our society. In fact, essentialist thinking is so pervasive that we grow up learning essentialist ideas about sexuality without even knowing that this perspective has a name and that there is an alternative view. We simply learn and accept these ideas as truth.

There are two major parts of sexual essentialism. The first is the belief that sexuality is a natural, inherent aspect of the self.

Sexuality as an Internal Drive

The notion of sexuality as a force within the individual finds expression in a number of ways. The idea of the sex drive is one of the most common. Most sex researchers and theorists over the last one hundred years, including Sigmund Freud, Alfred Kinsey, and William Masters and Virginia Johnson, have assumed an inherent sex drive. They may disagree over whether the source of this drive is physical or psychological, whether it comes from genes or hormones or from deep emotional influences. But they are agreed that sexuality is an insistent, internal force.

. . . .

Essentialism

- There is an internal, probably biological sex drive or instinct.
- Sexuality is universally expressed throughout different historical times.
- Sexuality is universally expressed across different cultures.

. . . .

It is important for educators to reexamine the notion of the sex drive because this belief contains such a compelling image—that there is a powerful force that drives our sexuality. Sexual instincts supposedly cannot be ignored; they will push to the surface and demand release. Because these urges and impulses are allegedly located in our bodies, this particular aspect of essentialism is also sometimes called *biological determinism*. The biological self drives the sexual person.

We live in a society that is suspicious and fearful of sexuality. Not surprisingly, then, many people imagine this powerful, inner force to be uncontrollably dangerous. Although both men and women have been viewed as aggressively sexual in different historical periods, currently this is particularly true of male sexuality. In a 1950s sex education text, *Toward Manhood*, Herman Bundesen wrote that sexuality, "like hunger, is one of the driving forces of life. It will not be denied. . . . There is no primitive impulse that can work more lasting harm on others, if uncontrolled, than the sex urge."[1] In a familiar refrain, he warned that girls should not tempt or seduce a boy, who might simply be unable to control the "lewd devils" that possess him—his sexual drive.

Although it might seem outdated, this particular essentialist myth about the nature of male and female sexuality still exerts a powerful cultural influence. The often repeated idea that men are naturally sexually aggressive while women are sexually passive reinforces myths that it is a woman's responsibility to tame or control the powerful male sex drive. It has taken decades for the contemporary women's movement to dislodge the popular idea that rape results from an uncontainable explosion of male sexual drive and to rightfully reframe rape as an abuse of male power, a social rather than an individual problem. Essentialist ideas are so culturally ingrained that this effort has still not completely succeeded. In 1989, for example, a man charged with raping a woman who was wearing a white lace miniskirt without underwear was acquitted because, according to the jury foreman, she "asked for it," while he reacted like any red-blooded American man.[2]

Since sexuality education reflects dominant ideas in the culture, it is not surprising that essentialist ideas about the sex drive permeate the field. Sexuality texts typically link the sex drive with hormones and suggest that there is a biological basis to the ways in which women and men prefer to be sexual. One contemporary text makes this argument quite boldly: "Within the male the sex drive is more specific and direct. It tends to be isolated from feelings of love and affection and directed more towards orgasm. Within the female the sex drive is more diffuse and is related to feelings of affection. Indirect stimuli such as sexual fantasies and provocative pictures have a much greater effect on the male than the female."[3]

Embedded in this argument are two common essentialist themes: (1) there are universal differences between male and female sexuality, and (2) these differences are the result of biological factors that constitute the sex drive. Although there has been intense debate and serious challenge to these ideas, they continue to be taught to new generations of students as though they were factual.

Contemporary sex researchers, like Masters and Johnson, have exerted a powerful influence on our ideas about sexuality. They have reinforced essentialist thinking through their insistence that sexuality is a natural force present in all of us at birth. But they have attempted, in many ways quite successfully, to reframe its nature. They cast the sex drive not as the "lewd devils" of an earlier age, but as a positive, healthy instinct. By insisting that sexuality is an inherent and natural drive, researchers like Masters and Johnson hope to convince us to appreciate rather than suffer shame over sexual thoughts, feelings, and behaviors. Don't feel guilty, sex researchers urge us, because your sexuality is a normal expression of a natural, inner sexual drive.

Essentialist ideas about an internal sexual drive or instinct, therefore, can be expressed as either negative or positive. The sexual force might be viewed as primitive, dangerous, and potentially overpowering. Or it can be seen as natural, normal, and healthy. We see these tensions in contemporary discussions about sexuality.

Some people, for example, believe that sexual orientation is the result of an inner biological or psychological drive (See Chapter Four for more on this subject.) And this essentialist belief, which has been hotly debated over the last twenty years, has been used both to support and condemn homosexuality. One writer who argued on behalf of lesbian and gay rights because it is "normal and natural" said, "From a psychological perspective an action is considered natural if it originates from an impulse or drive. . . . A substantial minority of human beings have an instinctive tendency to fulfill same-sex desires. . . . If, then, 'natural' is defined as that which is instinctive and freely acted on without restraint, same-sex feelings and attractions do indeed seem to be quite natural for a significant proportion of the human population."[4] But those who condemn homosexuality have used the same argument for their opposition. As one writer claims, we don't think everything that is "natural" is positive. This parent, who opposes teaching about homosexuality in the public schools, wrote, "Even if researchers like Simon LeVay discover that homosexuality is predestined by our genes, this affords us nothing: many forms of cancer and other autoimmune disorders derive from our genes, as well."[5]

Essentialism in the Media

The media commonly disseminate and reinforce essentialist ideas about sexuality. One example is a column printed in the *Boston Globe* on Gay Pride Day that drew outraged responses. An excerpt from this article shows how the columnist, Jeff Jacoby, uses essentialist ideas to argue that homosexuality is nothing more than a biological urge. Jacoby wrote:

What unites the gay paraders . . . is a characteristic utterly and consumingly physical: sexual orientation. It is *precisely* the demands of their bodies that pull together the tens of thousands of Gay Pride marchers who would otherwise have little or nothing in common. . . . The marchers' unifying attribute, the singular feature without which there would be no Gay Pride parade and no Gay Pride Day, is—being gay. They are defining themselves in terms of something bodily: carnal desire. And not just defining, but acclaiming. . . . Rejoice? In the swerve of their sex drive? That is not ennobling or uplifting. It is coarsening, and a little dehumanizing. The point is not that homosexuality is good, bad or neutral—that's a different column—but whether the essence of our selves is merely the total of our thirsts and desires.[1]

Jacoby has clearly made an essentialist argument here by reducing the complexities of sexual identity to an inherent sex drive or carnal desire. This article is an example of how essentialism can be used to argue that certain groups, identities, or sexual practices are pathological. Jacoby argues (even while denying that he does so) that homosexuality is both an inherent sex drive and one that is inferior by being "coarsening" and "dehumanizing."

[1] Jeff Jacoby, "CNN's Odd Juxtaposition," *The Boston Globe,* 16 June 1994. Reprinted courtesy of *The Boston Globe.*

Essentialist, biological explanations can therefore cut both ways. Modern sex researchers like Alfred Kinsey often used an essentialist argument—whatever we see in nature is normal and natural—in order to challenge sexual rules and taboos. But many, like the parent above, use essentialism to persuade others that nature only intended us to engage in certain sexual behaviors and that variations from nature's path are morally wrong.

Debates about adolescent sexuality also show how, in essentialist thinking, the alleged inner sex drive can be viewed as a force that is either positive or negative. Because teenagers are fresh out of puberty it is easy to see them as driven by hormones to engage in sexual activity. Some people still agree with Bundesen, who wrote that the adolescent sexual urge, like "lewd devils," is an overpowering force that adolescents must be taught to control.[6] Others argue that teen sexuality is simply a natural part of development. As one parent recently wrote, "A healthy interest in sex is part of the maturation process, and no matter how often we 'just say no,' some kids are going to succumb to experimentation. It's in the genes and hormones."[7] Both perspectives are essentialist because they view sexuality as an internal, natural force; they simply differ in whether this drive is dangerously powerful or a healthy expression.

We can see, then, that this first aspect of essentialism—the idea that sexuality is a deep internal drive—is a common theme in current discussions about sexuality. This is not surprising since, as I said earlier, essentialism is our culture's dominant framework for thinking about sexuality. In addition, sexual essentialism is reinforced by a significant development in the area of sexuality—that of medicalization.

Medicalization is a process by which a growing number of social issues are "taken over" by the medical profession and consequently are framed as health problems. Drinking, drug use, teen pregnancy, gambling, and violence are experiences that have been medicalized, so that we now think of them in terms of health and disease. We commonly speak, for example, about an "epidemic" of violence and the "disease" of alcoholism.

Over the last one hundred years, medical professionals have increasingly dominated discussions of sexuality. Whereas earlier, philosophers and religious leaders had been the experts, by the late nineteenth century, doctors began to define sexuality as a health concern. They invented the categories of different sexual experiences that are now so familiar to us, such as homosexuality, heterosexuality, transsexualism, and transvestism. And they created a language of sexual disease, conveying such concepts as impotence, preorgasmia, and sex addiction. It is now common to think of sexuality as a health issue, especially with growing concern over sexually transmitted infections like human immunodeficiency virus (HIV). Sex education is often taught in school health curricula, and nurses are often the instructors.

By framing it as a health issue, medicalization reinforces our tendency to think of sexuality as an internal drive. Although this is not true in many cultures, European-American culture considers health and illness to be an individual, biological experience. Unlike Native American or some Asian cultures in which disease is thought to spring from a lack of social or spiritual harmony, European Americans conceive of illness as an individual problem. Something inside of ourselves has gone wrong. The source of disease is thought to be a "bug" or some other outside invader that penetrates inside the individual person to cause illness, rather than a social problem such as the health impact of toxic wastes, pollution, or food additives. Experts who have medicalized sexual issues—for example, diagnosing frequent sex as "sex addiction" and infrequent sex as "inhibited sexual desire"—often look to the brain or hormones for the source of this "disease" rather than examining how our ideas about appropriate levels of sexual activity come from social norms.[8] It is clear, then, that applying medical ideas about health and sickness to the area of sexuality simply strengthens our already familiar belief that there is an internal and individual sex drive.

Sexuality and Biology: A Look at the Research

The body is a central focus in sexuality education. Sexuality education texts are filled with information on the roles of hormones and genes in our sexual lives. Moreover, newspapers, magazines, and scientific journals proffer enthusiastic accounts of the relationship between our biological and sexual selves. But how accurate is this information? Does biology play as strong a role in sexuality as many recent studies would claim? How might sexuality educators most accurately teach about biology? There are important resources to help sexuality educators evaluate these questions.

We hear a great deal these days about genes and genetic influences on our behavior. Researchers of late have been arguing that there is a genetic basis for such varied problems as alcoholism, mental illness, violence, and even smoking. Based on twin studies, some scientists have claimed that sexual orientation, specifically homosexuality, is largely genetic.

Harvard biology professor emerita Ruth Hubbard has written a lively and informative evaluation of contemporary genetic research. Hubbard is a knowledgeable critic who explains, in lay terms, how genes operate and then proceeds to criticize current research on a number of grounds. She points out flaws in the design and interpretation of numerous studies and shows how most claims of genetic influence are "a mix of interesting facts, unsupported conjectures, and wild exaggerations of the importance of genes in our lives."[1] Hubbard is essential reading for sexuality educators because she gives us information and analytic tools that allow us to demystify and evaluate this work for ourselves.

Scientists have made sweeping claims about the role of hormones on our sexuality ever since the birth of endocrinology in the early years of this century. In her book *Raging Hormones,* Gail Vines examines these various claims, including those that allege a hormonal basis for homosexuality and assert that estrogen and testosterone form the basis of female and male sexuality. Like Hubbard, Vines is critical of these overly broad claims about biology. She shows the ways in which the supporting studies are biased and how they play into larger social and political ideas about women and sexual minorities.[2]

Mariamne Whatley's work is critical reading for sexuality educators as they evaluate the implications of biology for teaching about sex. Whatley specifically examines how various texts present ideas about hormones and other physiological factors. She points to how a large number of texts distort information on hormones, and she provides concrete suggestions for educators on how to present physiology more accurately in the classroom.[3]

All of these many critics show how scientific studies, along with coverage of them in the popular media, mistakenly lead to a view that biology is the major influence on our sexuality. While offering rigorous methodological criticisms of the research, the critics place the studies in a larger historical context to show that, far from being neutral, they are part of a larger political climate in which claims about biology are being used for a range of social purposes.

[1] Ruth Hubbard and Elijah Wald, *Exploding the Gene Myth* (Boston: Beacon Press, 1993), p. 4.

[2] Gail Vines, *Raging Hormones: Do They Rules Our Lives?* (Berkeley: University of California Press, 1994).

[3] Mariamne H. Whatley, "Biological Determinism and Gender Issues in Sexuality Education," *Journal of Sex Education and Therapy* 13, no. 2

(1987): 26–29; "Raging Hormones and Powerful Cars," *Journal of Education* 170, no. 3 (1988): 100–121; "Male and Female Hormones."

Sexuality as Stable Across Cultures and Eras

Finally we come to the second major aspect of essentialist thinking, and one that places important limitations on the development of multicultural sexuality education. This is the tendency to think of sexuality not just as an internal force but as one that is predictably stable and similar both across cultures and throughout different historical times. The two essentialist ideas follow logically, for if one believes that sexuality is an inherent, individual drive, then it should unfold in humans in the same way, untouched by historical or social influences except in the most superficial ways. In this second aspect of essentialist thinking, we universalize the meanings, values, and belief systems about sexuality that are specific to our culture in the present.

We assume, usually without even thinking about it, that people in other cultures or in different historical periods think and feel the same way that we do about such practices as same-sex sexual activity or oral-genital practices. One example of this is the common essentialist assumption that the categories of heterosexuality and homosexuality are valid, timeless descriptions of human behavior and that heterosexuality represents the normal and natural development of the sexual drive. Some people, from this essentialist perspective, describe sexual activities between men and boys in ancient Greece as "homosexuality," even though the modern term had not yet been invented and their practices bore little similarity to the set of behaviors and identities we associate today with "homosexuality."

Together, these two assumptions—that there is an internal sex drive that is stable across time and cultures comprise sexual essentialism. We encounter examples of essentialism almost daily. Newspapers routinely report about scientists searching for a gene or hormone that causes homosexuality. These searches reflect an essentialist assumption that there is a biological basis, or sex drive, to the wish for same-sex sexual intimacy. Similarly, the notion that men are more sexually aggressive than women because they have a stronger sex drive is an essentialist idea. The presumption in some sexuality and AIDS education books that teenagers are "walking hormones" reflects essentialist thinking in that it assumes a biological sex urge and ignores the fact that widespread sexual experimentation during adolescence is not universal to all cultures and historical periods.

The Social Constructionist Challenge

Over the last two decades, historians and social scientists have developed a new perspective on sexuality that challenges essentialism. Sexuality, they argue, is not a fixed arena of human life that unfolds in a predictable way because of certain biological functions. Instead, the meanings, beliefs, values, and practices that comprise sexuality are often different in different times and cultures. This new perspective on sexuality is called *social construction theory*. The term suggests that sexuality is a product, or construction, of social and cultural influences during any specific historical time.

While essentialists look to the individual as the most important factor in explaining sexuality, social constructionists look to social and cultural influences. Most social constructionists minimize the role of a biological sex drive or instinct, and some deny that there is such a force. All agree that biology does not determine any particular form of sexual expression as normal or natural. Instead, sexual rules, or sexual scripts (see Chapter Two) shape individual behavior. These cultural rules don't inevitably determine our behavior; for example, one of the most dramatic findings of the Kinsey reports was the enormous gap between how the culture said individuals should act sexually and what people actually did. But cul-

ture offers us guidelines; most of us know the sexual rules of our culture even if we sometimes disobey them.

One term for the specific combination of sexual beliefs, practices, and rules is the *sex/gender system*.[9] The concept of the sex/
gender system has been an important one in the study of sexuality
because it reminds us that to understand individual sexual behavior we must understand how a particular society organizes and reg-
ulates sexuality in a specific period. Although essentialist ideas
falsely depict the sexual values and practices of dominant groups as
universal to all groups, in fact there is no sexual behavior, identity,
or belief system that is universally normal or natural. Cultures may
differ considerably.

Social constructionists argue that "sexuality" itself—the very
basis of what we consider to be sexual—can vary greatly from culture to culture. We cannot take for granted that cultures share the
meanings of sexual acts, or that there is even agreement about
whether an act is sexual or not. For example, although most Americans would agree that kissing is an erotic activity, the Mehinaku of
the Amazonian rain forests consider it a bizarre and disgusting
exchange of saliva.[10] While most people in the U.S. consider oral-
genital acts between men to be homosexual practices, such activity
is an acceptable, indeed required developmental phase for Sambian
males of New Guinea. The Sambia have no concept of, or terminology for, homosexuality and do not explain same-sex activity in
this way.[11] These examples represent more than simply the existence
of cultural variations; rather they show how the very foundation of
what we consider to be sexual may vary widely.

Dramatic differences can also occur within the sex/gender system of a single culture over time. One example from white, middle-
class U.S. culture is the dramatic shift in our ideas about female
sexuality. While many Americans accept as truth the notion that
men have a stronger sex drive than women, in fact our ideas about
male and female sexual desire continually change and even reverse

themselves. Popular ideas in the eighteenth century held that women were lustful creatures, almost out of control, who would tempt and seduce men. By the nineteenth century, experts said the opposite: men were supposedly more naturally sexually aggressive and women felt very little desire. This set of beliefs has persisted, although as we move into the twenty-first century, sexologists now say that they find no inherent difference between the sexual capacities of men and women. Social constructionists look at these reversals in expert opinion not as evidence of "real" changes in a female "sex drive" but rather as an example of how ideas change within a sex/gender system and how sexual rules shape our behavior by presenting us with certain sexual possibilities.

Social construction theory is an exciting advance in sex research because it has so many advantages over essentialism. It challenges old assumptions and argues that there are never any "universals" about sexuality. Constructionists question how sexuality is organized and symbolized in different societies. In particular, they stress that to truly understand an individual's sexuality we must understand the range of meanings he or she attaches to particular behaviors, feelings, and fantasies.

Social Construction Theory

- Sexuality is not universal either throughout history or across cultures.

- It is doubtful that there is an internal, essential sex drive or force.

- Biology plays a small role, if any, in determining our sexuality.

- Sexuality is deeply influenced and constructed by social, political, economic, and cultural factors.

- We must examine the specific meanings attached to sexuality at particular historical moments in particular cultures.

What About the Body?

We all grew up learning essentialist ideas about sexuality. So the social constructionist perspective can seem unfamiliar, abstract, and even irrelevant. In my classes and workshops, I've heard a range of responses from teachers, health care professionals, parents, and undergraduates. Many of them are excited by this new way of thinking about sexuality since it seems to fit more closely with their experiences, and they are intrigued by the possibilities social constructionism offers for their work. There is particular excitement about the way social construction theory opens up the area of cultural diversity. Others are skeptical, however, and wary of abandoning ideas that seem to have served them well in the past.

Perhaps there has been no more suspicion and resistance to social construction theory than with respect to biology and the body. Some think the essentialism–social construction debate is simply a variation of the nature-nurture conflict—an argument over the importance of biology versus that of the environment. They wonder why they have to choose a side instead of just staking out the middle ground. Surely, they think, both biology and the social world have an impact on our sexuality. But as we have seen, there is much more to the debate between essentialists and social constructionists than disagreement over a sex drive or the biological basis of sexuality. Moreover, social constructionists go much further than simply challenging the importance of the body's role in sexuality; as we will see, they raise questions about what we even mean when we talk about "the body."

In this society we have learned to view our bodies as a source of wisdom. However, this notion of the fundamental truth of biology is a belief that changes in different historical periods. Historians have noticed that these beliefs tend to be strongest during times of great social stress. At the moment, we are in a period of intense interest in finding in the body all the truths about who we are and how we act. An example of this is the Human Genome Project and other related efforts at tracking particular genes that are supposedly the origins of such practices as alcoholism, gambling, and homosexuality. Despite limited success and much criticism, these research projects receive enormous publicity and reinforce the popular notion that we can explain who we are through an understanding of our bodies.

So given this context, questions about the body are reasonable and important. What is the role of biology, if any, in our sexual lives? What about hormones and genes? What about the sex researchers who discovered that boy infants have erections at birth while the vaginas of newborn girls lubricate within hours? Doesn't that prove an inborn sexual drive? These kinds of questions have generated discussion not only among those resistant to social constructionism but among social construction theorists themselves who are debating the most accurate and meaningful way to account for biology.

Unlike essentialists, who look to the body in order to uncover truths about sexuality, social constructionists think the body simply affords us the physical potential for sexual practices. The body is a source of energy and a site of different parts and places, all of which allow the varied thoughts, feelings, and behaviors that we call sexuality to be enacted. But nothing is standard or universal about the way these energies and body parts operate. Instead, our social worlds teach us how to fashion the body's potential into what the culture considers to be a sexual person.

Some constructionists have compared sexuality to music.[12] Although the ear gives us the capacity to hear, the experience of the rich and varied combination of rhythms and tones that we call music is created by culture. We know that we need the ear to hear, but we don't think that our experience of music is based on the physiology of the ear, or that a preference for Bach over rap might be located somewhere in the brain. Courses on music don't focus on physiology, and people who are unmoved by music don't believe that their indifference stems from a physical problem with their ears. Our need to locate the source of our sexual selves in our bodies says less about any biological truths and more about how cultural anxieties about sexuality have remained focused on the sexual body.

Social constructionists adamantly reject arguments based on a supposedly natural or divine plan for the body—arguments that are no doubt familiar to sexuality educators. For example, some people say that heterosexuality is natural because male and female genitalia were built to fit together ("God made Adam and Eve, not Adam and Steve"). Or they object to anal sex because, supposedly, the anus wasn't designed for penetration by a penis. Constructionists would counter that these arguments work backwards in attempting to justify cultural biases by claiming a biological rationale for them. Obviously the body is capable of enacting a wide and varied range of practices that we call sexual. These are considered either acceptable or deviant based solely on the social meanings attached to them, not because God or nature had intentions about how the body should be used.

It is useful to recognize that the body itself is neither as stable nor universal as some believe. The body, in some ways, is itself a social construction. This is so in several ways.

First, we have learned that the body comes first; we are born with a fixed anatomy and physiology that then influences everything else. But there is growing evidence that the body is changeable and reacts to aspects of our social world. For example, stress changes body chemistry, and experiences such as severe childhood trauma seem to alter the makeup of the brain in complicated ways. These studies suggest that we each live in a social body, that what happens to us may well affect our body as much if not more than our body affects what happens to us.

Second, our experience of living in our body is profoundly affected by our social worlds. Cultures differ in the importance they attach to such specific body parts as breasts, buttocks, necks, ears, or eyes. Beliefs about beauty, which exist in every culture, can make one feel energetic and exuberant or awkward and uncomfortable in one's body.

Those who don't fit our particular culture-bound ideals, such as disabled, obese, or very short people, may feel burdened by their bodies.

Finally, scientific ideas about the body and how it works have often been shaped less through rigorously empirical methods than by social and political influences. For example, in the late nineteenth century, as both women and African Americans were launching movements for equal rights, scientists put forth theories about how both groups were physically different, and inferior to, white men.[13] Some believed that women were developmentally stunted and therefore more suited to domestic roles as wives and mothers. African Americans were said to have smaller brains, less intelligence, and more innate capacity for physical work, making them, of course, ideally suited for hard labor if not slavery. Alleged physical inferiority became a rationale for denying minority groups equal rights.

Political influence on representations of the body continues in the twentieth century. Sex researchers William Masters and Virginia Johnson admitted that their belief in gender equality shaped how they designed and reported their research on the physiological similarities of men and women in the human sexual response cycle.[14] And researcher Simon LeVay has said that he was convinced even before he began to look for the cause of homosexuality in the brain that he would find it. So these scientific portraits of the physical body, supposedly objective and true, are really pictures that fit with particular social and political beliefs of the time. They are constructions that will look as obviously biased to those who look back one hundred years from now as the nineteenth-century depictions of women's and African Americans' physical inferiority look to us now.

Questions about the role of the body in sexuality are not easily laid to rest. Indeed, as this section suggests, it is not always clear what "the body" even means—or that it means the same thing to all groups at all different times. Yet social constructionists would likely agree that biology plays a small role in our lives as sexual people. And for sexuality education, a field in which the body has been so central, this suggestion carries important implications.

Sexuality Education and Social Construction Theory

Sexuality education has been slow to recognize social constructionist perspectives. In part, this is because the field approaches sexuality as a health issue, and we have already discussed how medicalization reinforces the essentialist claim that sexuality is individual, internal, and timeless. But also, since social construction theory challenges the idea of universal truths, it doesn't offer its own. Instead, it encourages us to ask questions. As a result, I have heard teachers complain that it seems too abstract or difficult to apply to their work. However, social constructionism can be very concrete and pragmatic with regard to sexuality education.

Social construction theory has an especially important role to play in sexuality education in the area of cultural diversity and awareness. Because essentialists assume a stable sex drive, they can easily ignore culture or, at best, treat differences as simply minor variations on a fairly universal theme. We are all familiar with the kind of educational strategy in which only the beliefs and practices of dominant groups—for example, white heterosexual men—are considered. It is an outgrowth not of malevolence but of an essentialist view that assumes a great deal of sexual consistency. In contrast, a social constructionist approach insists that we target an intervention, such as a class or brochure, to fit the beliefs of specific cultural groups.

Sexuality educators should be particularly aware of this challenge to the idea of sexual universals, because so much underlying research is based on a biomedical, essentialist perspective. Most texts, for example, incorporate the work of scientific researchers. These studies are often based on very homogeneous samples (only white people who, in the case of Masters' and Johnson's studies, are mostly middle class and educated), and their conclusions are applied to all groups. So sexuality education materials may present findings as universal that are really specific to a particular group. It is encouraging that the recently released comprehensive study of sexual behavior, the National Health and Social Life Survey, was conducted by researchers who take a social constructionist approach to sexuality.[15]

Social construction studies help us understand that there are many areas related to sexuality in which cultural groups differ. Some examples are sexual beliefs and practices (is there acceptance, for example, of teenage pregnancy or anal sex?), the acceptability of sexually explicit language (does the term *gay* make sense, or should one say, "men who have sex with men"?), ideas about the purpose of sex (is it simply for reproduction, or is pleasure acceptable?), the relationship between sexuality and gender (is there a double standard?), and the role of the family (is there a tradition of an extended, involved family network?). Our educational strategies will be much more effective if our approaches are consistent with our audience's worldview.

The essentialist assumption of an internal sex drive has shaped sex education for over one hundred years. Here, too, a constructionist approach can improve educational strategies. Nowhere is this clearer than in the area of adolescent sexuality. When we assume that teenagers, especially males, are acting on the basis of sexual urges, our education emphasizes strategies for self-control, ways to channel their drives, or skills to make them safer because they will inevitably act on these impulses. This is the basis for "just say no" or more liberal "just use a condom" approaches. In addition, sexuality education texts that attribute sexuality to hormones often reinforce rigid gender roles by making broad arguments about biological causes for characteristics as diverse as sexual interest and aggressivity, sexual identity, career interests, and cognitive skills in such areas as math.[16]

Social constructionists don't assume that adolescents are driven by sexual instincts. Instead, they recognize adolescent sexuality as shaped by a range of factors from gender, race, and ethnicity to social class and sexual identity. The meanings that teenagers attach to sexuality and relationships will vary based on the many messages they receive from their social worlds. Some adolescents, particularly white males, receive powerful cultural messages that encourage frequent and aggressive sexual activity. Others, often European-American middle-class females and first-generation Asian-American males, get messages of sexual restraint. Instead of being driven by hormones, adolescents are operating from a range of sexual scripts. Like all of us, teenagers fashion their sexual ideas, expectations, and willingness to act on the set of cultural options available to them. If we understand those scripts, we can craft educational messages that they can more easily hear.

By now it must be clear that the content and effectiveness of sexuality and AIDS education is profoundly shaped by one's underlying theoretical perspective on sexuality. Sexuality education is a product of our culture and so has been dominated by essentialist thinking. As we have seen, this paradigm both distorts our ideas about sexuality and limits us in our ability to speak to diverse audiences. Social construction theory, on the other hand, asks that we know about the sex/gender systems of our audiences and that we target our programs for them. This perspective assumes we are social actors and that culture shapes our sexual beliefs and practices.

Sexuality may be complicated, but it does not defy understanding. I hope to demonstrate throughout this book that social construction theory is a tool that can help us develop richer and better programs to understand sexuality more thoroughly.

2

Cultural Theories, Cultural Practices

Sexuality education has been slow to address cultural diversity. The combination of essentialist theory and medicalization has led educators to attach overwhelming importance to individual drives and behaviors in sexuality. Culture, when mentioned at all, has been discussed simply to add exotic flavor. Sexuality education texts may, for example, describe the sexual practices of South Pacific tribes or other native peoples but then provide no cultural framework that would allow students to understand the deeper implications relative to human diversity. This sends a message about the "strange" customs of "foreigners" as compared to the "normal" practices of "Americans" (usually cast as a homogeneous group).

The AIDS epidemic has helped change this emphasis on individual sexual drives and behaviors by underscoring the need for culturally specific education. The groundbreaking HIV prevention work taking place in particular communities—for example among gay men, intravenous drug users, urban women, and the African-American community—contains powerful lessons about culture and sexuality. These programs show us in a tangible way that sexual definitions, meanings, and symbols are culturally constructed and that safe-sex campaigns are most effective when they are designed and targeted for different groups. However, while many educators now agree that programs must address cultural differences, there has been little discussion about what "culture" actually is, how it works, and how to develop effective multicultural sexuality education.

In the absence of such discussion it is easy for educators to rely on strategies that, while familiar, may be limited. This is the case with one common method of addressing cultural diversity at conferences or workshops: the multicultural panel. These panels usually consist of speakers from a range of communities—for example, African American, Latino, Asian American, and Native American—who address such issues as AIDS and safer sex from the standpoint of their culture. These efforts are valuable in their emphasis on the importance of difference, and I've organized several of them myself. However, it is worth examining their drawbacks, since such limitations plague other multicultural projects as well.

Multicultural panels set culture apart or make it different. This happens in two ways. First, the multicultural panel is often the only context in which diversity is mentioned, and other topics continue to be addressed from the perspective of dominant groups. Although this is happening less often now, it can still be the case that some events, except for the panel on diversity, are dominated by middle-class, educated European Americans. Second, the composition of these multicultural panels implies that only "minorities" constitute a culture. Panelists might be women, lesbian or gay, or from communities of color. This reinforces the myth that culture is "out there" away from the mainstream; that such dominant groups as European Americans, heterosexuals, and men don't have a culture; or, more importantly, that they are the universal standard, and everyone else is "different." These panels also implicitly suggest that cultures are homogeneous and so any one member can speak for the whole group. The point here is not to condemn an effort that can be useful, but to use it as an example of a strategy that raises important questions about the definition of culture and how it works.

Defining Culture

The precise definition of culture is a problem that has occupied anthropologists and sociologists for over a century. For the purposes of sexuality education, it is probably most useful if I give a broad, working definition of culture and then more carefully look at how these theories have changed and become more complex. Culture is the set of historically created worldviews, rules, and practices by which a group organizes itself. It serves as a blueprint or map to help us negotiate our daily lives. Cultural logics—things we take for granted as common sense—are woven throughout our existences. Culture shapes and constructs sexuality on the levels of what we believe to be sexual, what we know as the rules for being sexual (when, with whom, how), and, some would argue, even what we feel as sexual.

Before we turn to theories of culture, however, it is important to acknowledge that in the past decade the term *culture* has become part of our popular language. We use it loosely as shorthand for any group that seems to have some commonalities—for example, "youth culture," "rock culture," and "sports culture."

The casual use of this term is usually not challenged, unless it is attached to a group that, for whatever reason, is controversial. One relevant incident for sexuality educators was the bitter debate over including lesbian and gay families in the Children of the Rainbow multicultural curriculum in New York City in 1992. Although many people supported the curriculum and the notion of lesbian and gay culture, some opponents claimed that gay people were sick and deviant individuals, not members of a culture. I mention the Children of the Rainbow controversy here because the questions it raises about culture—what it is, which groups count as cultures, who gets included in multicultural education, and who makes these decisions—are at the heart of our challenge as educators.

One significant aspect of the Children of the Rainbow debates was the argument that some groups have an authentic claim to being a culture while others do not. For example, one parent protested, "They're teaching my child that being gay is on the same level as being Puerto Rican." His objection is based on a traditional idea that culture is transmitted generationally and that it is a set of shared patterns based on such seemingly biological characteristics as race and ethnicity.

This argument rests on ideas about culture that were once common among social scientists but have since evolved. Until the late 1950s, behaviorism dominated the social sciences, and culture was defined as patterns of behavior, actions, and customs. This definition included preferences in, for example, music, food, and clothing. In the Children of the Rainbow debates, supporters and opponents argued about whether or not lesbians and gay men have a history of shared behaviors. The notion of race and ethnicity as the basis of the most viable cultures rests on the early-twentieth-century concept that these categories are biologically based rather than socially constructed. In this view, racial and ethnic cultures are stable and permanently marked by physical characteristics passed on through generations. We will see how these ideas are limited as we examine more contemporary ideas about the nature of culture.

As reliance on behaviorism eroded in the social sciences, ideas about culture shifted. Anthropologists argued that culture is made up not just of shared behavior patterns but also of shared information, knowledge, or symbols. This broader notion suggested that people of a specific cultural background would have more in common than their preferences in music or food; they would share a more diffuse way of approaching and understanding the world. They would share a particular logic.

But this more comprehensive definition also had limitations. The idea of a shared cultural logic implied that cultures are more homogeneous and stable than we now know them to be. Currently, cultural theorists emphasize internal contradiction and multiplicity in cultures. Rather than being systems in which values, language or slang, subjective beliefs, or symbolic systems are universally shared, cultures are fragmented and multiple. For example, although some research suggests that there is a high level of intolerance toward homosexuality among African Americans, there are certainly many who are open and accepting of gay people. The view that cultures operate unevenly is more accurate; it is also more complicated for us as educators, since we must hold open the possibility of different and competing worldviews even within one cultural group.

Cultures in Practice

Using the basic notion of culture as a blueprint or map, there are several elaborations that are important for designing effective, culturally specific sexuality education.

Cultures construct but do not determine our behavior. Individuals learn the rules of their cultures and are shaped but not inevitably determined by them. In other words, we are not simply robots acting out cultural rules. While we can never be outside of the influence of our culture, our feelings, attitudes, and practices also reflect idiosyncratic aspects of our individual experiences and backgrounds. This is as true for sexuality as for other cultural areas. In a process that is not fully understood, we internalize sexual beliefs, value systems, and rules for practice. But we are not bound by these cultural maps. For example, premarital sexual intercourse was against the rules of the dominant culture for much of this century, but many people both participated in and enjoyed this activity.

Cultures are not static but dynamic. Although we can think of culture as a blueprint or set of somewhat stable rules, these rules evolve and change. Cultures are flexible entities; they respond to historical and social changes. For example, ideas about masturbation have changed radically in the last one hundred years. In the late nineteenth century, physicians believed that masturbation caused a range of ills, both physical and emotional. Masturbatory insanity was a diagnostic category. Not surprisingly, then, cultural rules forbade masturbation. Currently, however, doctors and sex researchers regard masturbation as a neutral, even healthy, practice. Virtually no one, even those who disapprove of masturbation, believes that it causes insanity or other dire effects. While it may not be entirely accepted (consider Surgeon General Joycelyn Elders's firing for suggesting the teaching of masturbation in schools), masturbation is a common topic in popular magazines, television, and the movies. The cultural rules have changed.

This potential for cultures to change and evolve is important for sexuality educators. Increasingly we realize that campaigns for behavior change—safer sex, for example, or contraception use—can only be effective if they help to bring about a shift in cultural norms, for it is difficult for individuals to change their sexual behavior if it puts them at odds with their culture. The problem for educators is that cultures don't change rapidly or easily, and we do not understand the precise mechanisms by which to bring about shifts in sexual mores. Nevertheless, it is useful not only to think about the sexual content of cultures but to see cultures as engaged in an ongoing and active process of constructing and reinventing sexual logics.

Cultures are not monolithic and homogeneous but internally contradictory. Blanket statements about cultural norms (for example, "the expression of sexual pleasure is acceptable among European-American women" and "it is unacceptable for Latinas to show an interest in sex") are often inaccurate. Tensions and contradictions exist within cultures. Saunders has expressed this as the difference between an ideal, dominant culture that may often be male defined (where, for example, women should be pure and chaste) and a counterculture in which there are different options at the level of real experience (where under some circumstances women can be highly sexual).[1]

Cultures are internally complex, and there may be gaps between the dominant cultural message and an individual's socialization into it. So although a tendency among middle-class European Americans in the late twentieth century has been the growing acceptability of sexual pleasure, we still find pockets of sexual shame, fear, and danger among many of the women. Individuals may also actively resist cultural messages. For example, there are specific arenas in which Latina women have some latitude to express sexual pleasure despite negative cultural rules, and there are ways in which women demonstrate resistance to restrictive sexual norms.

This contradictory aspect of culture puts us in a complicated position in the classroom. Although we know that cultural logics can be pervasive and powerful, we must also look for areas of internal tension or resistance. This paradox requires us to make generalizations about cultures while simultaneously being aware of the fragile nature of our assertion. Cultural generalizations are always vulnerable to challenge.

One reason for cultural contradiction is that *cultures are fractured along many dimensions*. Even within a culture there are divisions and differences according to such factors as race and ethnicity, gender, social class, level of assimilation, sexual identity, and age. When we make cultural generalizations, it helps if we can be specific about the group to whom we are referring. For example, because of the pervasiveness of double standards (although the particulars may vary), gender is an especially important dimension of sexual difference within cultures. Therefore, if we are examining premarital sexual practices of African Americans, Asian Americans, or European Americans, it makes a big difference whether we are discussing males or females. In this example, the effects of socioeconomic class also allow for great variability within groups.

Cultural assimilation is a variable in sexual norms of ethnic, immigrant groups. Assimilation refers to the extent to which one cultural group has taken on the beliefs and practices of another; usually the minority group integrates the logics and characteristics of the dominant culture. Acculturation is the process by which immigrant and host cultures affect and bring about change in each other. In the late twentieth century, assimilation is a more complicated issue; given the international distribution of U.S. cultural products, from television and popular music to clothing, most immigrants enter this country already familiar with dominant American cultural practices. In this country, degree of assimilation may affect the sexual beliefs, attitudes, and practices of an individual member of an ethnic group. For example, teachers who work with adolescents may notice that Haitian-American and Chinese-American teenagers are sometimes at odds with their parents over such issues as dating and sexuality, because the youth have adopted some of the dominant cultural logics while the parents still adhere to more traditional rules of their culture.

Individuals have multiple cultural identities. If cultures are internally divided, it follows that individuals within cultures will identify with a range of groups. For example, a person who is an African American will also have an identity based on gender, sexual identity, and socioeconomic class. Therefore, if we compare a middle-class, heterosexual, African-American man with a poor, African-American lesbian, not only might they have very different cultural logics and practices but they will be in different structural positions in terms of discrimination. While they both might experience oppression based on race, the woman would also be vulnerable based on gender, social class, and sexual identity.

Within cultures, then, individuals may occupy both dominant and nondominant groups, depending on the various groups with which they identify. Many people have some combination of identities that are dominant (European American, heterosexual, middle and upper class, male) and some that are nondominant (female, lesbian or gay, poor or working class, racial and ethnic minority). However, there are some—like the African-American lesbian mentioned above, or the white, middle-class, heterosexual male—whose identities are completely dominant or primarily vulnerable to oppression.

Multiple and intersecting cultural identities may put individuals in complicated positions. Sometimes the identities may leave one feeling divided, as might a gay male who is a practicing Catholic, because the norms of each group are at odds. Individuals are sometimes forced to choose whether to favor one identification or another. For example, psychologist John Peterson describes how racism in the gay community and homophobia in the black community contribute to conflicting dual identities for black men who are gay. Each culture has different norms concerning sexual identity. Peterson suggests that this conflict is managed differently by men who choose to primarily identify with the gay community ("gay black men") or the black community ("black gay men").[2]

Although individuals might find it a relief to emphasize one identification, it is difficult to be forced to ignore other important aspects of one's identity. In this country, unfortunately, movements for social change tend to be organized around a single identity. Analyses of racism, sexism, and homophobia have become increasingly visible. Analyses of people with intersectionalities—two nondominant identities—have been less frequent. So, for example, in the discussion of sexuality and sexual harassment during the Anita Hill–Clarence Thomas hearings, we heard a familiar narrative based on racial discrimination ("high-tech lynching") and another based on gender oppression (sexual harassment and abuse). But law professor Kimberle Crenshaw has argued that there was not a well-known political analysis that could encompass both gender and race for Anita Hill, given her intersectional identities as black and female.[3]

Everyone has a culture, even those in dominant groups. This is an obvious but ignored aspect of culture. Culture, as it is used in such terms as *multicultural* or *cultural diversity*, often refers only to nondominant groups, to those who are somehow different from the majority. So women, people of color, non-Christians, lesbians and gay men, and poor and working-class people are thought to have culture. On the other hand, men, heterosexuals, European Americans, Christians, and the middle and upper classes are not presumed to have culture. They are the norm. They occupy unmarked, supposedly empty categories that nevertheless define the standard against which everyone else is compared and inevitably judged different.

In our programs, if we treat only "minority" groups as a culture, we reinforce the sense that dominant groups are neutral and universal, that they are "above culture." One key aspect of privilege for people in these groups is that they are in a social category that is supposedly invisible but nevertheless defines what is "normal." It is important, therefore, to identify certain beliefs and practices as specific to dominant groups such as European Americans and heterosexuals just as we identify other norms with people of color and lesbians and gay men.

Culture is not biological or essential but socially constructed. The same theoretical insights about essentialism and social construction theory that we discussed in regard to sexuality have shaped contemporary debates about culture. Scholars argue that cultures and identities organized around such social categories as race, ethnicity, and gender are not essential or biologically based but invented and given meaning in ongoing social and political processes. In other words, it is not biology that gives rise to certain patterns, practices, and logics based on gender or skin color. Rather, these categories of gender and race are given particular meanings that change over time.

The United States has a long history of defining race as a biological category, with groups other than European Americans considered inherently inferior. The belief that race and racial culture are based on essential and immutable characteristics is widespread. But critics are challenging this notion (see Chapter Three). They point out that humans have such mixed and overlapping origins that the separation of groups by discrete physical traits is arbitrary and imprecise. For example, at different historical times Italian Americans and Latinos have been categorized as both white and nonwhite. Racial categories are only "real" because of the social meanings they have been given, not because of seemingly biological features such as skin color. Skin color, sociologist Stuart Hall argues, has nothing to do with blackness. "People are all sorts of colors. The question is whether you are *culturally, historically, politically* Black."[4] Race is an identity that people are not born with but must assume in an ongoing process of identification.

These new ideas about the construction of culture have important implications for sexuality educators. First, they remind us that an individual's level of identification with a culture is an ongoing process, not a biological given. We can't assume, to paraphrase Stuart Hall, that a particular student who is sitting in our class identifies with black culture(s) simply because she has black skin.

Second, social construction theory underscores that any sexual differences one might identify based on categories like race, ethnicity, or gender are social in origin, not biological. For example, working-class men do not "naturally" avoid masturbation. There is nothing biological to explain early ages of sexual intercourse among black men and women. Any patterns in a culture have historical, social, and political origins. They were invented by social actors and therefore can, and likely will, be reinvented and changed. Third, cultures have more or less recognition and privilege because of social factors, not biological ones. No culture is inherently more authentic or superior.

In our hierarchical society, some cultures are valued more than others. Our society maintains a powerful system of structural inequality. Groups that are nondominant based on race, ethnicity, gender, sexual identity, and class have less social, political, and economic power. This system affords power and privilege to some groups at the expense of many others.

Power differences show up in sexuality education in several areas. First, most sex research includes only dominant groups, from which generalizations are made about everyone's sexual belief systems, attitudes, and practices. For example, sexuality educators still use the data from the Kinsey reports to generalize about sexual behavior, even though those studies were based only on a European-American sample. In addition, sex research among communities of color tend to focus on problem areas—for example, teenage pregnancy and sexually transmitted infections. Finally, sexuality education materials frequently reinforce cultural bias. For example, in an analysis of photographs in sexuality texts, Whatley concludes that adolescents of color are most often depicted in photos that illustrate topics of sexual danger or immorality.[5]

Culture and Operation

- Culture is a set of rules or guidelines that influence individual behavior.

- Culture may be manifested in values, belief systems, practices, symbols, language, and fields of knowledge. Culture may be experienced as "common sense," or a cultural logic.

- Culture shapes but does not determine our behavior.

- Cultures are dynamic, always changing.

- Cultures are internally complex and contradictory.

- Cultures are fractured along many dimensions, including those of gender, class, and sexual identity.

- Individuals have many cultural identities.

- Everyone has culture, even dominant groups.

- Cultures are socially constructed.

- Some cultural groups have more power and privilege than others in our society.

This discussion of culture's internal contradictions, fragmentation, and social constructedness leaves us with the question of how best to develop a multicultural approach to sexuality education. If, for example, cultural categories are fluid and unstable, how do we even begin to address the possibility of group differences? And if individuals have multiple cultural identities, how can we determine the extent to which particular group norms have shaped their sex/gender systems? These are difficult questions that cultural theorists have not answered, and they may never be fully resolved.

Meanwhile, as sexuality educators, our approach to culture must be complex. We must be able to manage the potential ambiguities of culture. We cannot sidestep them by acknowledging cultural categories but then emptying them of all content or significance. This approach—"we're all the same under the skin" or "I don't care what color someone is"—is what Frankenberg calls color evasiveness and power evasiveness.[6] In sexuality education it could take the form of a move back to essentialism—for example, telling an audience, "there are certain biological truths to sexuality that we all share."

This strategy fails to address the social importance of culture in our society as it affects access to power and resources, and it ignores real differences in the construction of sexuality among various groups no matter how fluid they might be.

What is left for us if we avoid the approach that treats culture as stable and determining ("Asian Americans can't comfortably talk about sex") and the strategy that dismisses culture ("sex hormones are color-blind")? The middle ground is to be tentative and cautious. We explicitly recognize cultural diversity because we want people to be able to see themselves in our discussions. Just by pointing out that there are differences, we can help more people feel included, even if we haven't mentioned their particular cultural group. But our generalizations in a classroom will be partial, not universal ("some Asian Americans" or "certain black middle-class men"). We can always qualify or elaborate on our comments about culture and sexuality.

Our approach to cultural identities is similarly precarious. It can be useful to think of identities as "necessary fictions."[7] We acknowledge that, given how our society is organized, individuals need to locate themselves in particular cultural categories. These categories are important in the United States, and although there are some who insist they hate to be labeled, we can't simply deny a perspective (for example, saying "race doesn't exist; we're all one human race") without falling into the power-evasion trap.

On the other hand, these identities are "fictions" not because they have no social reality but precisely because they are a product of culture; they are categories we have invented and given meaning. Cultures are not biological imperatives that carry with them unchangeable characteristics. So we must be wary of treating culturally invented categories like race or sexual identity as though they are groupings that are universally and biologically stable.

Our approach to culture, finally, takes the form of an ongoing question. We assume that sexual meanings, and consequently practices, will be different among the many individuals in our classrooms.

And it is possible that some of those different meanings form patterns based on cultural group. But our assumptions end there. We hold in mind the possibility of difference, and it is useful if we have some knowledge of particular sex/gender systems so that we can imagine what some of those differences are. But we don't know how fully any particular student identifies with her cultural group. Or how other identities, such as gender, might interact. Or how her family's beliefs might conflict with their cultural norms. All of these intangibles give rise to questions we can integrate into our lessons. It is this very questioning—allowing students their own voice—that opens up the space in classrooms for cultural diversity to be recognized.

Learning the Culture's Sexual Rules: Script Theory

Culture interacts with sexuality in complicated ways. A number of questions arise when we recognize both sexuality and culture as social constructions. How do cultural differences shape the sexual thoughts, feelings, and behaviors of individuals? How do we learn to be sexual? How do we integrate the cultural messages around us into a set of sexual rules? Why are some messages more powerful than others, and why do some people make different sexual decisions than others? The honest answer to these questions is that we don't fully understand these processes.

Constructionists insist, however, that we learn to be sexual in the ways we learn anything else. Although sexuality might seem to be a special aspect of human life with a different set of rules, this is not inherently so. Sexuality is only unique because, as a culture, we have decided to set it aside and treat it differently than any other part of our lives. The process of becoming a sexual person is not an unfathomable mystery. It is something we continually learn from the world around us. Let's look at a few days in the life of one popular television adolescent as a way of examining some social constructionist theories on how we become sexual.

Angela is the fifteen-year-old protagonist of a current popular television show, "My So-Called Life." This show follows the lives of several adolescents—most of them European American—and the parents of Angela as they all confront problems at home, school, and work. In one episode, Angela faces an important sexual milestone: whether to have intercourse with her boyfriend, Jordan. This would be her first experience of sexual intercourse, while Jordan, we learn from one of Angela's friends, has been with many other girls. In the first scene, Jordan pressures Angela to "pick a place" where they can go and have sex (in keeping with the language of the show, I will use the term *sex* as a euphemism for intercourse).

How does Angela make her decision? The episode depicts her as totally engrossed in the process, looking for information wherever she can find it. Suddenly, for Angela, sex is the only worthwhile topic of conversation. Watching her, we see how her sexual decision making is a complex activity that is shaped by influences like the media, family, experts, and friends. She is learning the cultural rules about sexuality and fashioning them into rules for herself. One way of thinking about this social process is through the theory of sexual scripts.

Sociologists William Simon and John Gagnon have developed scripting theory from a combination of sociological and psychoanalytic theories.[8] Script theory suggests that becoming sexual is a lifelong process in which individuals learn cultural expectations about sexuality that they shape into their own particular patterns. Cultural meanings infuse our sexual desires and feelings; social expectations permeate the cues we use during sexual interactions. Even the term *script* suggests how sexuality is both profoundly social and performative. Sexuality takes shape in interaction between oneself and the social world.

Simon and Gagnon identify three levels of sexual scripting: cultural scenarios, intrapsychic scripts, and interpersonal scripts. *Cultural scenarios* are collective patterns that specify appropriate sexual goals, objects, and relationships. They are rules for how, when, where, and why to be sexual and whom to be sexual with. We learn these scripts from the dominant culture, but there are also sexual rules and belief systems that are specific to nondominant cultural groups. For example, African Americans and Asian Americans will learn the dominant cultural scenarios, those of European Americans, but also the rules and logics of their own cultures. Sometimes these cultural scripts will compete or contradict.

But we do not simply act out cultural scenarios, because we carry with us the influence of our own particular personalities, life histories, and experiences. This internal world of desires, fantasies, and wishes makes up our *intrapsychic scripts*. It is this personal narrative of sexuality and desire as shaped by the family and by cultures that has been the subject of psychoanalytic theorists, starting with Freud. It is important to point out that intrapsychic scripts are not biological drives. They are not the opposite of cultural scripts but are, in fact, shaped by culture.

Interpersonal scripts are patterns of interaction that allow us to function in sexual situations. They are usually fashioned from some combination of cultural and intrapsychic scripts as well as from the imagined expectations of the partner. There may be circumstances where interpersonal scripts quite directly reflect both cultural scenarios and intrapsychic scripts. But usually things are much more complicated, as individuals attempt to negotiate sexual situations while balancing both external and internal worlds. Nevertheless, interpersonal scripts help us to be sexual with others, even though most people are not consciously aware of them.

We can see examples of the three levels of scripting operating as Angela grapples with her decision. First, let's examine the level of intrapsychic scripting. It is more difficult in a film to have access to an individual's inner world, her intrapsychic script. But there is some evidence of Angela's internal process, her plans and fantasies at this moment in her sexual development. At the beginning of the episode, Angela has clearly reached a moment in her life when she is coming to terms with the meanings of having sex. She walks down the hall at school ruminating to herself: "I couldn't stop thinking about . . . the, like, *fact* of it: . . . That People Had Sex. That they just *had* it; that sex was this thing people . . . *had*. Like a rash. Or a . . . rottweiler. Everything started to seem like . . . pornographic or something.'"[9] We see here how Angela's internal process is still social; she is thinking about her own sexuality in relation to that of other people. She considers what and how other people might be sexual. She passes two teachers and muses about how they each have sex, and maybe even with each other! This speculation prompts a wave of self-criticism: "I am, like: The sickest person."

Like many adolescents (and even adults), Angela is preoccupied with sex. When she reveals this to her friend, Brian, we see how intrapsychic scripts (her ongoing thoughts, plans, fantasies, and desires) can be at odds with cultural scenarios (in this example, the rule that tells us that boys are more interested and obsessed with sex than are girls). In this scene, we also see how Angela is responding internally to the cultural expectation (and her own experience with Jordan) that boys only want sex, and we see how Brian challenges this.

ANGELA: Nothing happened to me personally I'm just . . . I just think it's kind of sad. That's all. About boys.
BRIAN: What about boys?
A: How they only care about . . . you know. Getting you into bed. Or something. I mean, don't they?
B: Not all boys.
A: I mean, I think about it. All the time. But . . .
B: Wait, you *think about it. All* the *time?*
A: Brian! Yeah, shut *up,* boys don't have the monopoly on thinking about it.
B: They don't?[10]

Cultural expectations affect our intrapsychic scripts, then, but they don't overpower them. Angela can talk about her evolving inner sexual life, and we also see some evidence of her wishes and desires for Jordan in scenes where there is clear sexual tension between them.

Second, let's look at the cultural level of scripts. Cultural scenarios are sexual rules, the "common sense" or logic of sexuality. But just because we know the rules doesn't mean we will obey them. We are social creatures, but we are also individual actors. Cultural scenarios are not easily ignored, however. They are powerful in that they serve as standards for what is seemingly right and moral. In part they are enforced because when we adhere to them we feel normal and natural, in tune with our culture. So individuals can resist or disobey cultural scenarios, but there may well be a cost. Cultural scenarios may be contradictory (sexuality educators are fond of pointing out the paradox of the two cultural messages, "sex is dirty" and "save it for someone you love"), and individuals who identify with nondominant cultures can be influenced by different sets of scripts.

Since our sexual lives are influenced by cultural scenarios, Angela searches around her for the rules about intercourse. What do other people do and how have they made their decisions? Experts are an important source of sexual information, and they shape our sexual beliefs and expectations. One way that they do this is by giving out information about what is "normal" behavior. Angela pursues this source of guidance with her doctor when she goes for a flu shot. She tells the doctor she has a question for a school project. "It's a question about percentages of what's normal. You know, in terms of, what people actually do. I mean, people my age. I just need to see some . . . statistics." Here, Angela hopes that knowing what most other girls her age are doing will help her decide. If she does the same thing, maybe she will feel "normal." Later with her friend, Sharon, she watches a self-help video—another source of sexual messages. They giggle as the couples on the film have intercourse while a sex therapist intones advice in a serious voice: "No human desire is shameful or abnormal."

Peers, who often reflect back to us various cultural norms, are another source of sexual learning. Angela talks to her friends. She mistakenly assumes one of them, Sharon, has decided to stay a virgin, and when she realizes her error, Angela blurts out, "You had, like, intercourse?" "Like, constantly," Sharon replies. The message here is that it's no big deal, Sharon has crossed this line. Later, Angela, hoping for further guidance, asks her, "So how did you, like, decide?" Sharon, however, can only recall that one day she decided she was "ready." Angela's Latino, gay male friend, Rickie, has another perspective on sex. He tells her that sex "should be like . . . a miracle. Like: Seeing a comet or feeling like you're seeing one."

It's important to point out that while this show entertains us by showing Angela's exposure to different cultural scenarios about sex, it also serves to reinforce these messages for all the viewers. Television can be a very powerful tool for teaching cultural norms. Adolescents tuned to this show hear, along with the fictional Angela, a range of different attitudes toward having sex. They hear the two girlfriends express nonchalance (Angela's other friend, Ray Anne, says, "It's so tragic to see her making this whole big deal over this thing that's, like, over in three seconds"), while Rickie and Brian take the decision more seriously. The show upholds the cultural expectation that boys (Jordan) pressure girls (Angela), who are more reluctant, to have sex. But it simultaneously undermines gender stereotypes through the viewpoints of the characters of Sharon, Ray Anne, Rickie, and Brian. Sexual pleasure doesn't figure prominently for any of the characters, including Angela's parents, who, in a parallel plot, worry that their sex life is "mechanical."

Parents, schools, religions, and advertising are also powerful vehicles for teaching cultural rules about sex. While none of these influences figure prominently in this particular show, Angela has likely been exposed to competing messages from all of them. However, as a middle-class, European-American adolescent, she is largely surrounded by the rules and logics of the dominant culture.

Third, we come to the level of interpersonal scripts. In interpersonal scripts, we draw on cultural rules and our internal fantasies and desires (as well as our fantasies about the expectations of the partner) in order to interact with someone. Interpersonal scripts can be smooth and practiced or, as is more often the case, awkward and undeveloped.

Sexuality educators often target the level of interpersonal scripts for intervention. It is mapped as the key site for behavior change. We do this, for example, when we teach adolescent girls "lines" they can say when pressured for sex by adolescent boys. One popular book contains supposedly witty comebacks for girls; for example, if he says, "I won't hurt you and I'll pull out in time," the text coaches her to say, "I think I'll pull out of this relationship fast!"[11] Safer-sex education is dominated by intervention at the interpersonal script level. One brochure is filled with rejoinders women can use to persuade male partners to use a condom. For example, if he says, "They look ugly," she might say, "Come here, big boy. I love the way you look in that color."[12]

Most of the time this targeting at the interpersonal script level happens without an awareness of script theory—especially Simon and Gagnon's elaboration of the three conceptual levels. But interpersonal scripts appear to be the clearest level on which behavior occurs; something is happening between two people, and it would seem to be the obvious moment to intervene. Most educational strategies address cultural scenarios only minimally, if at all, and virtually ignore intrapsychic scripts.

Given the emphasis educators place on interpersonal scripts, it is absolutely stunning to watch the interaction between Angela and Jordan. Like perhaps most adolescents, their direct communication about sex is virtually nonexistent. They don't ever approach the possibility of intercourse as a joint decision. Neither one can discuss his or her own feelings, desires, fears, and conflicts. They can barely look each other in the eye. Their "conversations" on the topic consist of rolled eyes, shrugged shoulders, and disconnected, seemingly random phrases punctuated by long, yearning kisses.

Throughout the entire show, although Angela is internally obsessed and seeking out as much outside information as possible, she and Jordan share only a few mumbled references to "being together." Then they have a fight a few days after Angela breaks the plan they had to "be together." This is their most explicit interaction about having intercourse:

ANGELA: It's so hard to explain, because it's not gonna sound right, because . . . part of me really wants to.
JORDAN: This is the whole reason I didn't want to start this in the first place.
A: Why? Because you knew you wouldn't get sex? So. You'd just be wasting your time?
J: Because you don't *get it:* okay? You're *supposed* to. It's . . . *accepted;* it's *what you're supposed* to *do.* Unless you're, like: Abnormal.[13]

Devastated, Angela turns and walks off. (She's just been given another cultural message: girls who don't want to have sex are abnormal.) Then, although this isn't discussed either, they break up.

Script theory, by helping us to examine the three different levels of sexual learning and decision making, allows us to target our strategies differently. We can see that, if Angela had been coached in her sexuality education class with witty little rejoinders, it would have been totally ineffectual. For rejoinders to be even remotely useful, a conversation has to be happening in the first place. Angela and Jordan clearly need to develop effective interpersonal scripts, and the scripts must go beyond simple phrases like "just say no" or "use a condom." Angela and Jordan need to be able to communicate more deeply about sexuality, intimacy, and their relationship. Some classes have begun to integrate lessons and exercises on sexual communication.

Helping students to evaluate various cultural messages is also crucial. How, for example, does Angela sort out and respond to what she hears from her friends, her doctor, the video, Jordan, and her family? Finally, intrapsychic scripts receive little attention in the classroom. And, as we can see, Angela is obsessed with sex and with her decision about first intercourse. Studies show that adolescents crave discussion about their sexual feelings and decisions.[14] We must create the space for them to have this discussion.

In summary, then, sexual scripting theory carries important messages for sexuality educators. First, awareness of the multiple levels of sexual scripts allows us to work with the dynamic between cultures and individuals in a more complex way. In particular, it reveals the limitations of concentrating on the interpersonal level when all three levels are intertwined. Change at the interpersonal level, for example, cannot easily happen without cultural support and intrapsychic shifts.

Second, scripting should be understood as a powerfully constructed dynamic. Despite a popular association with the lines or roles in a play, scripts are not simply learned behavior that can easily be unlearned. Women do not fail to insist on condom use, for example, because they can't think of effectively snappy responses to men's refusals. Role playing and rehearsal are certainly useful behavior-change components of sexuality education. But ultimately cultural scenarios for both men and women must allow for women's power in sexual negotiations. And for lasting change, women need not just new interactive responses but strong inner feelings—intrapsychic scripts—that support sexual empowerment.

The interconnections among all levels of sexual scripting suggest a third concern for sexuality educators: sometimes when we ask people to change their interpersonal scripts we put them in conflict with their cultural scenarios. This could doom the intervention, if individuals refuse or are unable to change interpersonal negotiations in which they are not supported by cultural norms. Conversely, if the intervention succeeds and the individual does change an interpersonal script, he or she might be left in an unpleasant, conflictual, or even dangerous situation. For example, one unanticipated consequence of successful HIV and AIDS education for women was that when some began refusing sexual activity without a condom they were beaten by their partners.[15] Their sexual assertiveness was at odds with certain cultural norms of male dominance and female submissiveness.

Fourth, although the three levels of sexual scripts are interrelated, they are not necessarily congruent within the individual. We know, for example, that people's intrapsychic scripts—their desires, fantasies, wishes—are often in conflict with cultural norms. Sometimes this can affect interpersonal scripts. Adolescent pregnancy, for example, is sometimes a problem for young women who are beginning to recognize their lesbianism (intrapsychic script) but are terrified by social discrimination (cultural scenario). They engage in sexual activity with men as a way to try to "prove" their heterosexuality, but they fail to protect themselves during intercourse. Disjuncture among script levels is quite common and helps explain a range of sexual conflicts.

Fifth, since individuals often have multiple and competing cultural identities, they must manage conflicting scripts. This was the case in the earlier example about the dual identities of black men who are gay and sometimes must resolve competing scripts by foregrounding either racial or sexual identities. Crafting effective programmatic modes of intervention for people with competing sexual scripts can be one of the most challenging tasks for sexuality educators.

Finally, although Simon and Gagnon don't specifically use scripting theory to discuss the role of cultural diversity in sexual learning, the theory is very useful for this purpose. It ensures a multicultural perspective. Since there are three levels of scripts, educators cannot simply focus on the interpersonal level. Cultural scenarios—the sex/gender systems of different groups, both dominant and nondominant—must be a major focus in our programs.

Behavior change is perhaps our most challenging and elusive goal. There is much that we don't yet know about how to help people change their sexual behavior. We do know that the process is complex and involves a focus not just on individuals but on their entire social universe. Script theory is one tool that allows us to do this.

• •

There are three levels of sexual scripts:

Cultural scenarios are collective patterns that specify appropriate sexual goals, objects, and relationships. They serve as guides for performance by narrating for us how, when, where, why, and with whom to be sexual. Another term for this might be *sex/gender system.*

Intrapsychic scripts constitute an internal world of desires, fantasies, and wishes. Intrapsychic scripts are not biological drives but are, in fact, shaped by culture. Intrapsychic scripts help us with sexual expression by managing and ordering sexual desires and fantasies.

Interpersonal scripts enable us to function in sexual situations. They are usually fashioned from some combination of cultural and intrapsychic scripts as well as the imagined expectations of the partner. Interpersonal scripts allow for coherent sexual interaction.

3

Constructing Race, Inventing Stereotypes

Race is one of the central social categories many educators think about when considering cultural diversity. We ask ourselves whether there are racial differences in certain sexual belief systems or practices. And if so, what do they mean for our curricula or our outreach efforts? Yet even as we grapple with the important challenge to develop programs that are culturally specific, a debate over race—whether it exists, what it means—makes our task more complex. The current disagreements among scholars over the concept of race have major implications for our multicultural work.

The Social Construction of Race

Briefly stated, these debates center around the usefulness of the term *race*. Whereas once scientists defined race as a fixed, biological category into which individuals could be neatly sorted, many now argue that the task of grouping people by physical characteristics is based less on objective biological variation and more on social and political influences. Race, these challengers insist, is a social construction.[1]

The idea that race is a neutral, tangible category based on biological characteristics is long-standing. One might argue that racial groups as we categorize them today, and the individuals—whites, blacks, American Indian, Eskimo, Aleut, Asian, or Pacific Islander— who fit into these groups, are obviously distinct. The linking of such physical characteristics as skin, hair, eye color, and amount of body hair with geographical region is seemingly observable. One scientist noted that if dropped by parachute into Nairobi one could easily determine whether one was there or in Stockholm. It is silly, these scientists assert, to say that there are no races.[2]

However, to say that "race" is socially constructed is not to say that there are no differences in physical characteristics among groups of people. But scientists have pointed out that only 6 percent of genetic variation can be explained by race, and that most variability occurs *within* population groups, not *between* them.[3] Therefore, a social constructionist approach would question why there has been such intense attention to such a relatively small realm of difference. It encourages us to question biological determinism and examine how physical characteristics have been given social meanings throughout different historical times.

In this view, race is political, not neutral and objective. Sociologists Michael Omi and Howard Winant show how even the earliest scientific efforts to classify different racial types were influenced by political interests—for example, the need to justify slavery and deny property rights based on the alleged inferiority of certain groups of people.[4] Injustices like slavery and the Tuskegee experiment were rationalized on the basis of fictional biological differences between blacks and whites. Biological arguments that supposedly explain racial inequality continue to attract popular and scientific interest. The widespread visibility of the book *The Bell Curve*, which alleges that there is a genetic basis to lower intelligence levels and therefore a disadvantaged social position among blacks, is a recent example.[5]

. . . .

Racial Sexualization and Medical Research

One consequence of a social hierarchy in which some groups are valued more than others is the very real possibility for stereotyping and abuses of power. Medical research is one site where such discrimination can occur. Two examples, which carry profound implications for sexuality educators, are the Tuskegee experiment and research on AIDS in Africa.

The Tuskegee Syphilis Study was conducted by the United States Public Health Service from 1932 until 1972, in cooperation with the Tuskegee Institute in Alabama. Its goal was to study the effects of untreated syphilis on black men. Researchers recruited a sample of 600 black men, 399 of whom were in the late stage of syphilis when the study began. Although the experiment was originally designed to last only six to nine months, investigators saw what they imagined to be an important research opportunity, and the study ultimately lasted for forty years.

There are several important aspects of the Tuskegee experiment that reveal how deeply racism shaped this study, from its conception to its conclusion. First, the goal of the study was to observe the natural history of syphilis in black men and determine if race was a factor in its developmental course. This notion rested on old myths that blacks were inherently different in anatomy (smaller heads, bigger penises among men) and neurology in ways that might alter the course of a disease or susceptibility to it. These ideas suggested that blacks' alleged physical and psychological inferiority and supposed sexual promiscuity were innate racial characteristics.

Second, the participants were treated like laboratory animals, not human beings. The men were deceived throughout the experiment. They were not informed of the purpose of the study, and those with syphilis were told only that they had "bad blood," a local catchall term for a variety of problems. In withholding this information the researchers allowed the disease to be spread throughout the black community. One of the most reprehensible aspects of the experiment was that, although there was no effective treatment for syphilis when the study began, when penicillin was invented and became the standard treatment in 1951, it was withheld from the subjects. Researchers made the decision to allow the disease to spread, unchecked, until the men died from it and could be examined in an autopsy.

Third, researchers within the U.S. Public Health Service not only continued the experiment but continued to support the idea and failed to question its ethics. The study ceased in 1972, but only after a public outcry arose in response to a story published on the front page of the *Washington Post.* In a 1992 PBS documentary, one of the researchers insisted, even then, that it was an important and legitimate study.[1]

While the Tuskegee experiment may be one of the most egregious examples of racism in sexual health care, it is certainly not the only incident. Women of color have been subjected to forced abortions and sterilizations. Lack of funding for clinics prevents many poor people from receiving education and services concerning sexuality. A recent report documented that doctors express negative attitudes and engage in discriminatory practices toward lesbian and gay patients.

Sexuality and AIDS educators working with cultural minorities may face understandable anger and suspicion as a result of these abuses. In fact, certain early medical approaches to HIV/AIDS simply perpetuated the racist sexualization of the Tuskegee experiment.

Medical and governmental responses to the AIDS epidemic laid bare the power of cultural stereotypes. Critics have detailed how homophobia and racism contributed to apathy by the Reagan-Bush administrations and a slow response by public health officials. As long as the epidemic was confined to "risk groups," defined in the early years as gay men, Haitians, and intravenous drug users (most of whom were people of color), officials paid little attention. This was revealed in a 1985 comment by Margaret Heckler, then secretary of Health and Human Services, who remarked, "We must conquer [AIDS] . . . before it affects the heterosexual population and threatens the health of our general populations." This was a stark reminder of our social hierarchy, that some cultural groups count more than others in our society.

Yet stigma and marginalization fueled far more than inattention; they profoundly shaped ideas about AIDS, where it came from, and how it is transmitted. In particular, the construction of AIDS in Africa

reveals the deep impact of racist sexual stereotypes. As they fashioned their ideas about the epidemic, medical researchers studying
AIDS in Africa drew on old and familiar associations of Africans with
promiscuity, sexual depravity, bestiality, and disease.

One early and controversial theory suggested that AIDS origi-
nated in Africa. This was, in part, based on virological research on a
retrovirus in African green monkeys. In the popular imagination, however, this hypothesis quickly took hold in a rapidly spreading urban
legend that was vaguely formulated but contained the elements of
monkeys, Africans, and sex. Not surprisingly, this inflamed both
African political leaders and African Americans, who rightfully heard
echoes of ancient stereotypes of Africans as apes and Africans having sex with animals. It was virtually impossible to do a speaking
engagement on AIDS in the late 1980s without being asked how
green monkeys had spread AIDS here from Africa. The insinuations
were clear; as Harlon Dalton wrote, black people kept asking him,
"What are they trying to say we *did* with that monkey?"[2]

Similarly, racist sexual stereotypes infused medical studies of
AIDS transmission in Africa. In conferences and research papers,
medical officials continually spoke of sexual promiscuity among
Africans, although they sometimes used the contemporary euphemism, "poly-partner sexual activities." One anthropologist wrote,
"Although generalizations are difficult, most traditional African societies are promiscuous by Western standards. Promiscuity occurs
both premaritally and postmaritally."[3] (Many readers will no doubt be
struck by researchers' use of the term *promiscuity,* since most sexuality educators abandoned the term long ago out of recognition of
how it unfairly stigmatizes and moralizes. Kinsey was alleged to have
pointed out the relativism of the term by saying, "Someone who is
promiscuous is someone who's getting more than you are.")

The focus on promiscuity was a common theme and shaped the
direction of both research and program interventions. As some critics pointed out, although certain sexual behaviors may have posed
a risk for HIV, the almost exclusive research focus on "promiscuity"

allowed other risk factors to go unnoticed. In addition, by describing promiscuity as a cultural norm for Africans, researchers ignored important contextual reasons for multiple sexual partners, including the fact that poverty resulted in separation of households due to labor migration: for survival, families have had to split up and relocate to separate areas, where both men and women might take other sexual partners. Cultural stereotypes yield only simplistic answers; a closer look at African life reveals a much more complicated picture.

The formulation of ideas about African AIDS is simply one example of the powerfully destructive historical legacy of racist sexual stereotypes. Researchers relied on these sexual myths about a cultural group and shaped their research agenda around them. Apart from being morally objectionable, this limits the quality and accuracy of the research as well as the effectiveness of educational programs based on these ideas.

[1] See James H. Jones, *Bad Blood: The Tuskegee Syphilis Experiment—a Tragedy of Race and Medicine,* rev. ed. (New York: Free Press, 1993).

[2] Harlon Dalton, "AIDS in Blackface," *Daedalus* 118, no. 3 (1989).

[3] Randall M. Packard and Paul Epstein, "Medical Research on AIDS in Africa: A Historical Perspective," in Elizabeth Fee and Daniel M. Fox, eds., *AIDS: The Making of a Chronic Disease* (Berkeley: University of California Press, 1992), 346–376.

. . . .

Not only are racial categories political but the categories themselves are unstable. Definitions of race are not standard and objective but are shaped by political considerations. For example, the categories themselves—the factors that determine race—have changed and continue to change over time. Different countries have different racial definitions. In Britain, "black" refers to all non-whites, including Asians and Afro-Caribbeans. Racial categories in some

Latin-American countries are so fluid that sometimes siblings can be classified in different racial groups. In the United States, the category of "white" is so rigidly enforced that anyone with a black ancestor is considered black. The U.S. has the "one-drop rule," in which anyone with even one drop of so-called black blood is considered black.

The task of taking the census has been fraught with group fighting over racial and ethnic classification. Native Hawaiians are arguing that they should be moved from the Asian or Pacific Islander status to the American Indian or Alaskan Native categories. Meanwhile, the Asian or Pacific Islander category contains a wide range of groups who have nothing in common. And the dilemma of how to classify Hispanics has been so complicated that the census committee labeled them an ethnic group rather than a race. The task of classifying a diverse but intermingled world of people is not simple.[6]

The idea that race is a biological fact has lead to the problematic belief in intrinsically different racial cultures. Increasingly, individuals are discussing their painful struggles with this myth. Reginald McKnight writes about the contradictory notions of what constitutes "blackness": "Many of us have assiduously searched for the essence of blackness and again and again returned to the inner self empty-handed. What does one have to be or do or believe to be truly, wholly, monolithically black? Some have suggested to me that the wearing of European clothing is unblack, while others have preached the Black Gospel while dressed like Young Republicans. . . . Some have insisted that marrying a nonblack spouse is unblack, while others have said, When you get down to it, we're all African."[7] In other words, there are no sets of thoughts, feelings, or behaviors that are intrinsic to particular racial groups. Like McKnight, we would find it fruitless to search for the essence of black sexuality, white sexuality, or any other pattern supposedly based on race.

Since race is a socially constructed and unstable set of categories, individuals respond to these classifications as social actors, not as passively defined objects. Some choose to identify with the racial category to which society would assign them, but they emphasize, as Stephen Carter writes, "Race is a claim. A choice. A decision. Oh, it is imposed too. The society tells us: 'You are black because we say so.' Skin color is selected as one of many possible character-istics of morphology used for sorting. Never mind the reasons. It is simply so. It is not, however, logically entailed."[8]

Others choose different categories, and they "pass" to the other side of the color line. This was true of many relatives of author Shirlee Taylor Haizlip, who writes of how they abandoned their black family members to pass for white. Haizlip went looking for those relatives and concluded her long search and her reunions with them with the realization of how, in fact, race is deeply constructed by social influences. She wrote, "I began the search for my mother's family believing that I was looking for black people 'passing for white.' And they did indeed pass. But what I ultimately found, I realized, were black people who had become white. After all, if you look white, act white, live white, vacation white, go to school white, marry white and die white, are you not 'white'?"[9]

If, then, race is an invented and unstable category, should we simply abandon the term? Some people have made this argument, saying that we are all part of just one race, the human race. But a social constructionist position on race does not advocate that we disregard the concept. In fact, this attempt would be counter-productive, if not impossible, in a society that is so structured around categories of race. Trying to be color-blind in a color-oriented world means that we've confused the biological instabilities of race with the very concrete social realities of racial inequality and discrimi-nation. Although "race" was invented, it still forces very real social consequences on individuals who happen to be classified as white or black. A social constructionist approach to race in our educational programs means that we recognize that racial categories hold impor-tant social meanings but that these meanings are not inherent or universal expressions of difference. Constructionist theory also insists that we look at the impact of racial meanings throughout history.

Race and Sexual Stereotypes

The work of sexuality educators is complicated by a historical legacy of racist sexual stereotypes. Sexuality has been a central domain in which dominant groups have exercised power over minority groups. The sexuality of certain peoples has been depicted as somehow primitive, uncontrollable, or radically different. This reinforces a belief in the inferiority of these groups as a way to justify their subordination.

Though centuries old, this dynamic persists. And the consequences linger, fostering understandable suspicion and anger among stigmatized groups. This is another dimension in which, in our society, cultural differences are not simply neutral but the bases for inequality. Therefore, it will not be sufficient for sexuality educators to simply incorporate culturally diverse perspectives into programs. We must actively confront the history of sexual stigma and its role in reinforcing unequal social power.

Cultures have different sexual logics or rules. And, as we have seen, these differences are not innate but are patterns resulting from a complicated social, political, and economic history. There is a complex relationship among dominant and nondominant cultures concerning sexual differences. For example, nondominant groups are not totally powerless; they can affect and shape the rules of the dominant culture. And they can carve out powerful zones of resistance to dominant rules. The remaining chapters in this book contain examples of the varied sexual meanings and logics applied to sexual life by nondominant groups. In this section, however, I want to show how the dominant culture has historically exercised the power to marginalize other groups by depicting them as sexually depraved and dangerous.

Many groups—for example, lesbians and gay men, mentally retarded people, and members of certain ethnic groups—have been and continue to be vulnerable to this tactic of marginalization. Racial difference, however, has been the site of probably the most entrenched and vicious sexual stigmatization. The powerful role that sexual stereotyping has played in subordination by race or color has a long-standing and visible history that clearly illustrates how this strategy operates.

Sexual stigmatization usually constitutes one of a constellation of alleged differences in a racial group. Winthrop Jordan documents how Englishmen, during the earliest European expansion into Africa in the sixteenth century, viewed the Africans as profoundly different from themselves in color, religion, and way of life and behavior, including sexuality. Englishmen began to translate the combination of such physical differences as skin color, hair texture, and facial features and such cultural differences as reflected in clothing, housing, and sexual behavior into the notion of African savagery. They described Africans as beastly; at a time well before theories of evolution, some suggested they evolved from apes.

This conflation of Africans with animals, although not widely believed, nevertheless contributed to a climate in which Africans were alleged to be sexually promiscuous and to engage in bestiality. African men were seen as dangerous to white women. In 1730 one traveler wrote, "At some Places the Negroes have been suspected of Bestiality with them [apes and monkeys], and by the Boldness and Affection they are known under some Circumstances to express to our Females; the Ignorance and Stupidity on the other side, to guide or control Lust; but more from the near resemblance [of apes] . . . to the Human Species would tempt one to suspect the Fact."[10] As Winthrop notes, this symbolic association between Africans and apes expressed the idea that Africans were lewd and depraved. As we will see, this theme has persisted regarding African-American sexuality.

Sexual stigmatization was central in the European expansion into North America. Two interrelated factors consistently underpinned this strategy. First, colonists read cultural differences of native groups as not simply neutral variations but as signs of inferiority. Second, this alleged inferiority served as a justification for European dominance, and in many cases eradication, of native peoples. Europeans saw it as their task to civilize the "savage" customs of the natives, at the same time that they were competing for land and resources.

Europeans encountered Native American tribes in every region in which they settled, from New England to Florida and Louisiana. Although the colonists saw themselves as entering an uncivilized wilderness, they were, in fact, invading communities and farmland long established by native tribes. Gradually Europeans eliminated Native Americans through direct warfare—the Pequot War, for example, in which seven hundred Pequots were killed by the colonists—or the dissemination of viruses to which the natives had no immunity. Epidemics such as smallpox decimated tribes: between 1610 and 1675 the Native American population dropped from 12,000 to 3,000 among the Abenakis and from 65,000 to 10,000 among southern New England tribes.[11] Although these epidemics were sometimes intentionally inflicted—for example, by giving natives blankets contaminated with pathogens—colonists interpreted the widespread destruction as divine intervention. William Bradford wrote, "For it pleased God to visit these Indians with a great sickness and such a mortality that of a thousand, above nine and a half hundred of them died."[12]

The colonists justified this savage behavior through their beliefs that the Native Americans were heathens who needed to be converted and civilized. Differences in sexual cultures served, for them, as powerful evidence for this assessment. Historians John D'Emilio and Estelle Freedman note that, although generalizations are difficult because there were variations among the many tribes, there were, in fact, many differences between the Europeans and the Indians.[13] Most native people, for example, did not associate sexuality with sin, guilt, and shame. Nudity was not uncommon, and many tribes accepted premarital intercourse, polygamy, and cross-dressing. Rape and prostitution were rare among Native Americans until the tribes adopted these practices from the Europeans. There were also, however, some similarities between Europeans and Indians, such as the rarity of contraception and abortion in both cultures.

But Europeans emphasized sexual differences and consistently depicted Native Americans as depraved. One missionary said of them, "Impurity and immorality, even gross sensuality and unnatural vice flourish."[14] It is clear that the description of native people as uncivilized sexual savages in contrast to the moral superiority of the Europeans served as a powerful rationalization for their domination and murder. Similar conflicts erupted in the Southwest, where white settlers who were colonizing native lands viewed Mexicans as "debased in all moral sense."[15] Again, differences in sexual cultures, such as a freer expression of desire among Mexican women, were used as evidence of inferiority and immorality.

This strategy was employed with a range of other groups over the next centuries. Anglo-Europeans consistently cast other racial and ethnic groups as sexual savages, the men uncontrollably dangerous and the women promiscuous. In the nineteenth century, for example, general social and economic anxiety prompted by rising immigration occasioned the widespread use of sexual stigmatization against minority groups. Racial and ethnic groups were pitted against each other, for jobs, resources, and respectability. For example, the Chinese were compared to the Irish, and both were compared to blacks. All of them were sexually demonized. The Irish were described as apelike savages pursuing "gratification merely animal," while the Chinese were cast as lustful and depraved.[16]

American blacks, of course, were thoroughly sexually stigmatized. As with ideas about blacks' inherent mental inferiority or inherent physical resistance to fevers and disease, the notion of black sexual depravity served to support the system of slavery and impede blacks' progress during the Reconstruction. Whites disregarded the sexual norms and customs of slaves and viewed them as either culturally or physically inferior. Ideas resurfaced about black sexual savagery. Black men were depicted as dangerous sexual brutes with a penchant for raping white women. Black women, who were routinely raped during and after slavery by white men, were seen as unrapeable and instead always sexually available. The black male rapist and the black female whore are enduring American myths by which "whites asserted sexual dominance as one means of insuring political and economic dominance over members of other races."[17]

Racist sexual myths have had an enormously negative impact on communities of color. During and after the Reconstruction, for example, the idea of the black male rapist fueled waves of lynchings in which black men, and sometimes black women, were viciously mutilated and tortured before death. These acts of terrorism were supposedly to protect "white womanhood" but in fact served to control and subordinate the black community. Similarly, the myth of the sexually lascivious, always lustful black woman reinforced ideas that blacks were animal-like, potentially uncontrollable, and certainly not deserving of full equality.

Paradoxically, characterizations of blacks as sexually accessible and dangerous in fact left them extraordinarily vulnerable. Black men, already viewed as rapists, could mount no believable defense to save themselves from lynching or, later, from execution. Figures from 1980 show that of the 455 men executed for rape since 1930, 405 were black men, most of whom were accused of raping white women.[18] On the other hand, black women could access little protection from sexual victimization. How could they be raped if they were always sexually available? A recent study revealed that, compared to white women, black women who are raped are more likely to assume that no one will believe them and less likely either to report the rape or seek treatment.[19]

Racial-sexual stereotypes infuse our social institutions and belief systems. The Anita Hill–Clarence Thomas hearings serve as one highly visible example of the ways that these ideas shape contemporary events. Critics complained that the hearings reinforced the myth of the oversexed black man ever "perversely concerned with the size, length, and place to put his penis, even on his way to the solemn and hallowed halls of the Supreme Court."[20] The testimony of Anita Hill was interpreted by certain Senate committee members to fit the profile of the sexually voracious black woman. She was cast as a man-hating lesbian or as a scorned and vengeful whore. Either way, the Senate committee dismissed her charges as insignificant and confirmed Thomas. Despite his victory, the hearings revealed the widely entrenched myths of black male and female sexuality.

The most negative effects of racist sexual stereotypes accumulate in daily activity rather than in the public theater of events like the Hill-Thomas hearings or the Mike Tyson rape trial. The effects are evident in three areas of particular importance for sexuality educators: social attitudes, health and education strategies, and social policies.

As we have seen, European Americans have circulated negative sexual stereotypes about communities of color since colonial times. These ideas evolve and change; for example, the explicit comparison of black sexuality to that of apes and other animals would be unacceptable today. Yet there is a remarkable historical consistency in sexual images of not just blacks but other people of color: oversexed (although in the case of Asian-American men, both oversexed and inadequate), dangerous, and prone to deviance and disease. Some of these myths—for example, black male sexuality driven by an enormous penis—are based in essentialist ideas. Others—the "hot" Latin lover, for example—have a supposedly cultural basis.

In both blatant and subtle ways, these stereotypes infuse social attitudes. They are often reinforced by the media. In their pervasiveness, racist sexual myths affect the dominant culture by repeating messages that can be learned and incorporated by individuals at a very early age.

Sexual myths profoundly shape the communities at whom they are directed. Black men, for example, may incorporate the image of sexual stud.[21] And, as we saw earlier, many black women who have been raped have been deeply affected by myths that they are always available for sex. The internalization of stereotypes about race and sexuality has a range of destructive consequences, from negative self-esteem to a justification for dangerous activities. One man, for example, used myths about his culture as an explanation for failure to engage in safer sex practices. "The Mexicans—we're not very preventive. It's in the culture. We don't pay attention."[22]

It is clear how education and health strategies can be affected by sexual stigmatization. Belief systems that individuals hold about the sexuality of European Americans and members of communities of color circulate throughout a classroom, even when unspoken. Teachers may target young black and Latino women for messages about birth control. As Whatley notes, sexuality education texts reinforce myths of the danger of black sexuality by including photographs in which blacks are frequently depicted as pimps or prostitutes.[23] White heterosexual students may feel that they are invulnerable to HIV/AIDS, that it is a problem only for stigmatized groups such as gay men and communities of color.

Educators confront the consequences of racist sexual stereotypes not only on the individual classroom level but structurally as well. There is, for example, little sophisticated research on sexuality in diverse cultural groups. Most research about sexuality in communities of color focuses on problems—for example, early pregnancy and sexually transmitted infections. This reinforces the idea that the sexuality of these groups is an area of danger to be contained.

These danger myths fuel health and social policy as well. Images of supposedly oversexual young black women indiscriminately bearing children underpin current efforts to reform or eliminate the welfare system. The fusion of black sexuality with disease has shaped the direction of both medical research on AIDS and educational initiatives (see Racial Sexualization and Medical Research).

Given this historical legacy, it is clear that sexuality educators face a larger task than the already considerable one of shaping effective multicultural initiatives and restructuring curricula. Students and teachers alike carry images and stereotypes about race and sexuality that are continually reinforced by the media, health and sexuality research, and government policies. If not made visible and challenged, these myths can sabotage the most comprehensive educational programs.

4

. . . .

Being Sexual:
Our Behaviors and Identities

Cultures differ in being sexual. One aspect of this is variability; culture influences attitudes, beliefs, and whether certain practices like oral and anal intercourse are acceptable. In his landmark sex research, for example, Alfred Kinsey found enormous differences between working-class and middle- and upper-class men in such behaviors as masturbation, petting, and premarital intercourse. Cultures privilege some sexual practices while rendering others less interesting or taboo.

Yet cultures exert an even more profound influence on sexuality than simply encouraging some practices over others. Indeed, culture determines our fundamental ideas about what is considered sexual or not sexual and how, when, and where such acts should be carried out. For example, some cultures code oral-genital behavior among men as sexual, specifically homosexual, while others do not.

Most significantly, culture infuses particular acts, categories, and identities with meaning. In sexual exchange, for example, a white, middle-class woman's exchange of sex for material goods within marriage carries different meanings than her selling of sex on the street. And among Latino men, one's identity as heterosexual is not destabilized by intercourse with other men if he is the "active" partner, the one who penetrates.

The cultural construction of sexuality poses a range of challenges for sexuality educators. We cannot assume that audience members agree with us, or with each other, about sexual codes and meanings. Intervention that is based on the presumption of universal systems of meaning and identity will inevitably be disregarded by those who hold different values and beliefs. The AIDS epidemic highlighted this dynamic when early prevention messages directed at the gay male community by outside public health officials failed for this reason. Gay men themselves were able to develop effective programs based on the constellation of meanings and symbols attached to specific acts within gay male sexual culture.[1] Similarly, women quickly recognized the need for very different AIDS education based on the specific sexual cultures of urban women of color.

There is a great need for more research on how sexuality is constructed and given meaning in different cultures. We don't even have sufficient data on the much simpler question of how specific practices, like masturbation and anal intercourse, vary among groups. There is a small literature, however, that can at least serve as a basis for considering cultural differences in being sexual and how they might influence sexuality education. This chapter will explore this topic as it relates to three areas: reproductive sexuality, nonreproductive sexual practices, and sexual identities.

The Meanings of Reproduction

Sexual meanings are constructed by cultures, and they also change over time. In the United States, there has been a shift in the dominant culture away from the notion—common from colonial times into the nineteenth century—that sexuality is almost exclusively connected with marriage and reproduction.[2] There is no longer the assumption, among most groups, that the sole or most important purpose of intercourse is procreation. Even among traditionally sexually conservative groups like Catholics, pleasure is now an acceptable outcome of marital intercourse.

Reproductive issues continue to assume enormous importance in our society, however. Debates over abortion and surrogacy reveal deep disagreements over the meanings of sexuality, pregnancy, and mother-hood. In addition, the concern about teenage pregnancy highlights questions about who should give birth and when is the best time. These deep cultural tensions illustrate that although reproduction is a biological act, it is also deeply social. Individuals, particularly women, face a range of reproductive decisions that include whether, when, and under what conditions to have a child; whether to con-tracept; and whether to abort. Each of these choices is freighted with cultural symbolism. And depending on social and material circum-stances, each of these choices may not be a choice at all.

Teenage pregnancy provides a good example of how social and cultural factors shape the meanings attached to reproduction. Ado-lescent pregnancy is a prime target of sexuality educators. Although there are deep disagreements over curricula, program comprehen-siveness, and values, educators seem to agree on the goal of adoles-cent pregnancy prevention. When cultural factors are inserted, however, this simple goal is seen to encompass a more complicated matrix of values and attitudes based on gender, social class, family structures, and access to material resources.

Since the 1970s, escalating cultural anxiety about the "epidemic" of teenage pregnancy has prompted a range of strategies to deter sex-ual activity or postpone reproduction among adolescents. Preven-tion of teenage pregnancy appears to be a worthy goal because it has been associated with so many negative consequences, including school dropout, low socioeconomic status, and neonatal mortality and other obstetrical risks.[3] However, it seems increasingly possible that these negative reproductive outcomes are less biologically determined—the result of childbearing at a young age—and more the result of social and environmental factors.

Social class clearly shapes patterns of adolescent pregnancy. Among both blacks and whites, teen childbearing is highest among those most socially and economically disadvantaged.[4] And although socioeconomic class is a major predictor, race also exercises an effect. One in a hundred black women from high-achieving, affluent, two-parent homes becomes a single teen mother compared to one in a thousand of comparable whites. Of low-income, poorly educated black women from a female-headed household, one in four becomes a teenage mother. The risk is one in twelve for comparable white girls.[5]

Policy researcher Arline Geronimus ignited a firestorm of controversy about adolescent pregnancy in the early 1990s. In reexamining the traditional data on teenage reproduction, she challenged the assumption of the universal destructiveness of adolescent pregnancy and childbearing. Geronimus emphasized that the negative consequences of teen reproduction are less the effect of biological age or the pregnancy itself and more the result of preexisting material circumstances. Teenage childbearing, she notes, "is a social response to disadvantage" that may, in fact, carry some advantages for poor women.[6]

This suggests that, because of material circumstances, the meanings of adolescent childbearing are different for poor white and black women than for middle-class white women. For example, poor adolescents are healthier than they are in their twenties, so childbearing may be less risky. Through early childbearing, women may be freed to find employment by their twenties and so have more ease in entering the workplace. Further, ethnographic research in the black community reveals a range of positive cultural factors that support early childbearing, including assistance with child care by the extended family and active involvement by the father and his family network.[7]

Geronimus's formulation is contested by some, who term it a defeatist strategy. They worry that policy makers will just give up on black adolescent girls if it is suggested that there are cultural differences that might support, and even lend advantage, to early childbearing. Conceivably, these different approaches can coexist. The point is to recognize cultural factors that might positively support decisions for early reproduction as well as cultural factors that block black adolescent girls from any other meaningful life option, thereby leaving pregnancy as the only path.

This reframing of the debate on adolescent childbearing is important in that it foregrounds the impact of race and class in teenage reproductive decisions and practices. Even if the focus of educational programs continues to be pregnancy prevention, programs will be much more effective when based on a cultural analysis of sexuality and reproductive decision making than on an essentialist model of drives and hormones. The latter urges teenagers to "just say no," while the former recognizes the need to understand the different meanings and symbolisms associated with the sexualities of adolescents in different racial, ethnic, and social positions. And significantly, a cultural analysis inevitably leads to improving the structural and material circumstances of adolescents so that their sexual and reproductive decisions are truly choices.

This is the approach taken by the Children's Aid Society's Adolescent Sexuality and Pregnancy Prevention Program in Harlem.[8] It is a model that "focuses on affecting young people not only individually but also in the context of their culture, family and community systems."[9] In addition to sexuality and family-life education, teenagers in this program receive medical services, tutoring, career planning, employment, and sports opportunities. In addition, all program participants are guaranteed admission as freshmen at Hunter College of the City University of New York. This program is the logical culmination of the awareness that adolescent reproductive behavior, among both boys and girls, is not just the end result of biological drives that must be controlled but also a complex system grounded in the social and cultural realities of day-to-day life.

Nonreproductive Sexual Behaviors

Social construction theory suggests that the same sexual act may have different meanings for different social groups. Or, in fact, one group may not even code that act as sexual. Further, sexual meanings and symbol systems change over time. Unfortunately, we have very little research that examines the sexual meanings of different cultures and the ways in which they change.

. . . .

Being Sexual: What Counts?

Kinsey didn't ask about it. Shere Hite did, but only wrote about it on the last page of her book. There weren't any questions about it on the newest, most comprehensive sex survey since Kinsey, the National Health and Social Life Survey (NHSLS). It is certainly part of the sexual script of the dominant culture in the United States. So why is kissing the orphan of sex research? Researchers ask about frequency of vaginal intercourse; they ask about oral and anal sex. In the NHSLS they even included a written questionnaire on masturbation that could be filled out in private. But they didn't ask anyone about kissing.

The absence of kissing is most likely a statement about what "counts" as sex in our culture. Indeed, kissing barely figures as a "base" in the popular baseball sexual metaphor; it is a fleeting stopover in "going all the way" toward the ultimate goal of intercourse. And this bias in dominant cultural values is reflected by sex researchers, who emphasize "the grand slam" but ignore the kiss. This research then reinforces ideas about which activities are important and which don't count.

There is certainly cultural diversity relative to kissing. In her essay "The Kiss," Leonore Tiefer documents variability both in what a kiss means and how it is performed. For example, she notes that the deep tongue kissing that is a familiar part of intimacy in Western societies is unknown or considered unhealthy or distasteful among certain African and South American societies. Kissing is virtually absent in the erotic art of China and Japan; indeed, the Japanese, who have no indigenous term for kissing, have recently adopted the composite: *kissu.* The Germans, on the other hand, have at least thirty different words for a variety of kisses. And although deep kissing is uncommon around the world, many cultures do practice some form of contact with the mouth, nose, or cheeks. For example, the Tinguians inhale with their lips next to a partner's face.[1]

Tiefer's summary was drawn from international cross-cultural data files. It would be interesting to know if there are variations in the nature and meaning of kissing among cultural groups in this country. There may well be gender differences, with kissing being quite important to many women while intercourse remains the main event for men. In her last-page discussion of kissing, for example, Shere Hite quotes many women for whom kissing is at least as important as intercourse, if not more so.[2] One challenge for sexuality educators is to examine how we omit discussion of kissing in curricula and to consider what message we send to our students by this omission.

[1] Leonore Tiefer, *Sex Is Not a Natural Act and Other Essays* (Boulder, Colo.: Westview Press, 1995), 77–81.

[2] Shere Hite, *The Hite Report: A Nationwide Study on Female Sexuality* (New York: Macmillan, 1976).

One study that is widely cited by social constructionists is the anthropological work of Gilbert Herdt with the Sambia people of New Guinea.[10] Herdt demonstrated that the act of oral-genital contact with the exchange of semen between men, which is commonly coded as homosexual in U.S. dominant culture, is not thought of as homosexuality among the Sambia. It is not even considered a sexual act but is, rather, a developmental "coming of age" ritual. This example is so commonly used because it graphically illustrates the danger of assuming that the sexual meanings of the dominant culture are universally shared.

We don't have comparable information about different cultural groups in the U.S. This poses a challenge for sexuality educators, for whom such knowledge would be crucial for effective program development. In addition, there is little data on variability in sexual behaviors among different groups. The information we do have about sexual variations is limited in that it only suggests frequency patterns—for example, that some groups engage in particular behaviors more than other groups. This neglects the important question of context, since the preferences and dislikes of certain groups are not random but are part of a web of values, beliefs, and meanings central to the culture. The frequency data tells us something is going on, but it doesn't tell us why.

Nevertheless, it is still useful to know if there are patterns of sexual behaviors that vary by culture. Certainly it is helpful for AIDS educators to know if particular groups practice certain activities more or less. We have only a small literature on this subject, so it is perhaps most useful to focus only on major themes.

The most groundbreaking sex surveys of this century were, of course, the reports on male and female sexuality conducted by Alfred Kinsey and his colleagues. The Kinsey reports are limited in several ways. First, they are dated, since they were published in the late 1940s and early 1950s. Second, they report only on white Americans. Third, they were based on a volunteer sample and so are not applicable to the entire population. However, it is still beneficial to look at Kinsey's findings. His data continue to be influential to this day, in part because his sample size was quite large (almost six thousand for each study) and because there is so little other research.

One of Kinsey's landmark findings for males was major differences in sexual behavior by social class. Significant variations occurred in choice of sexual outlet and in sexual technique. Those whom Kinsey called upper-level males masturbated more frequently and engaged in more petting but less premarital intercourse, homosexual behavior, or sex with prostitutes; they experienced more nocturnal emissions. The "lower-level" males were found to be more genitally oriented and very sexually active but revealed little interest in foreplay or erotic activities other than intercourse. Kinsey found that upper-level males were more tolerant of homosexuality, but lower-level males engaged in homosexual activity more frequently.

A portrait of striking cultural difference emerged in Kinsey's description of social-class patterns for males. He noted that upper-level men tended to focus on issues of morality and to rationalize their sexual activity according to notions of right and wrong. Lower-level males, by contrast, described their behavior in terms of what they considered to be natural or unnatural. Kinsey believed that these differences by social class resulted in cultural conflict and mis-understandings, as members of each group mistakenly assumed that their values and sexual patterns were universally shared. He empha-sized that this was cultural, not individual disagreement: "Conflicts between social levels are as intense as the conflicts between nations, between cultures, between races, and between the most extreme of the religious groups. The existence of the conflict between sexual patterns is, however, not recognized by the parties immediately con-cerned, because neither of them understands the diversity of pat-terns which exist at different social levels. Each thinks that he is in a conflict with a particular individual. He is, however, more often in conflict with a whole culture."[11]

Kinsey's data on the significance of social class in male sexual-ity were so powerful that they remain a point of comparison even today. We need always question how class might shape sexual pat-terns in every cultural group. And it is of particular interest to understand how class interacts with such other social categories as gender, race, and ethnicity. Although Kinsey failed to show such a dramatic impact of social class on women (the effects of gender were much stronger), this may have been a result of his methods. We do not have the data to confidently rule out a strong influence by class on the sexual patterns of women of all races and ethnic groups.

The National Health and Social Life Survey, published in 1994, supported many of Kinsey's findings about sexual behavior and social class.[12] The NHSLS, begun in 1988, is the most ambitious sur-vey since Kinsey's work. Although based on fewer people—nearly 3,500 as compared to Kinsey's almost 12,000—it is a representative sample of the U.S. population. Some findings of the NHSLS may be of limited value, however, because a small number of the ninety-minute interviews were conducted in the presence of a partner or other family member. This may have made some people reluctant to tell the truth about their sexual activities. Yet despite these limitations, the NHSLS will likely serve as a new yardstick by which we measure and evaluate the sexuality of the population.

The NHSLS found striking differences based on social class for both men and women. (The survey measured and reports education levels, which can be considered an indicator of social class.) For example, among men and women, the effect of education on masturbation was dramatic. Eighty percent of men with graduate degrees reported masturbating in the past year, compared to 45 percent of men who had not completed high school. The percentages of women who reported masturbating in the last year were 60 percent with graduate degrees compared to 25 percent among those who did not finish high school. More highly educated men and women reported higher frequency of masturbation than those who have less education. Many of these differences hold up for such activities as oral and anal sex as well. For example, 80.5 percent of men with graduate education reported a lifetime experience with performing oral sex compared to 59.2 percent of men with less than a high school education. These few examples indicate that there may still be validity to Kinsey's assertion about the differences in sexual cultures by social level.

Racial cultures may also affect sexuality. A consistent finding from sex research of the two decades, including the NHSLS, is of differences between the sexual behaviors and attitudes of white Americans and African Americans. There are important factors to consider before reviewing this data, however. First, there is a relatively small number of studies, their samples are sometimes small and non-generalizable, and they often ignore the effect of social class. Second, if there are differences in black and white sexual patterns they are, of course, neither inherent nor biological. Sexual differences emerge from a combination of cultural traditions and structural factors by which people have varying levels of power and resources.

One popular generalization is that blacks have a more liberal sexual culture than whites. Some sociologists have suggested that because of their particular social and historical circumstances, blacks have been less subject to moralistic restrictions and are therefore more liberal and direct.[13] In part, this notion is based on research that indicates that both black men and women were more liberal in sexual attitudes than whites, that black men experience first coitus at an earlier age than white men and have a greater number of premarital and extramarital partners, and that black women had an earlier age of first intercourse than white men and had more premarital sexual experience.[14]

A full review of the data on black and white sexual differences reveals a more complicated picture. The theory of black liberalism and permissiveness holds only if one views sexuality as intercourse-centered. Most studies show that blacks prefer genital intercourse, while whites engage in more varied behaviors.[15] Compared to whites, blacks of both genders are less likely to masturbate.[16] Black women are less likely than white women to participate in cunnilingus, fellatio, anal intercourse, and group sex.[17] Black men were less likely to engage in cunnilingus.[18] In addition, in contrast to earlier research, Wyatt suggests that black women experience more sex guilt than white women.[19] To characterize blacks as more sexually liberal in the face of these data reveals a striking bias about what kinds of sex really "count" and which are less important.

Cultural and individual sexual patterns change, and the data show this for black and white sexuality. Black and white ages of first sexual intercourse are becoming more similar, since the age among whites has been declining over the last fifteen years.[20] Sexuality educator Pam Wilson reports that she more frequently hears blacks discussing oral sex and sexual experimentation.[21] People may shift their sexual patterns after contact with other cultural groups. One black man described the changes in his sexual practices: "Now I didn't get involved in the oral sex until I was in the Navy. I didn't get into masturbation until I was in the Navy. There were a lot of things I didn't do. . . . [There was] pressure from the guys—these aren't white guys, these are black guys—'you ought to try [oral sex] sometime.'

So I tried it and I didn't like it. And I tried it again with my girlfriend and I didn't think she was gonna let me. And you try it again. By that time it's nothing."[22] In this fashion, then, the sexual pattern he had learned in a southern, black, strongly religious culture shifted with exposure to other cultures and practices.

In 1948, Alfred Kinsey emphasized the cultural variability of sexuality when he wrote that "there is no American pattern of sexual behavior, but scores of patterns, each of which is confined to a particular segment of our society."[23] These cultural patterns guide our educational initiatives by indicating that messages concerning prevention of pregnancy or disease should be constructed differently for different groups and that prevention strategies themselves might have to be different. An awareness of cultural differences is essential to sexuality education. But once again it should be emphasized that cultures are dynamic and shifting. Our assumptions about cultural patterns should be constructed with caution.

Thinking About Sexual Identities

There is a popular button that reads, "Don't Presume I'm Heterosexual." This message is meant to highlight difference in sexual identity, a difference that is often hidden. Lesbian and gay activists have, in the last several decades, challenged assumptions about homosexuality and rejected secrecy and invisibility, raising social consciousness about the range of sexualities and identities. This is a challenge with particular relevance for sexuality educators, because material and programs designed with a heterosexual assumption will simply be irrelevant, and even insulting, to lesbians and gay men.

Sexuality educators face a range of questions in this area. First, how do we teach to audiences in which different members are presumably heterosexual, lesbian, gay, and bisexual? Second, what and how do we teach about homosexuality and homophobia? Third, how do we teach about the broader area of sexual identities? Fourth, how do we integrate cultural analysis into lessons on sexual identity? As we proceed with this discussion, it is important to recognize that this topic is perhaps one of the most controversial and contested within the already embattled field of sexuality education. Nevertheless, most educators agree with the Guidelines for Comprehensive Sexuality Education issued by the Sexuality Information and Education Council of the United States (SIECUS), in which information on sexual identity is included as indispensable to sound sexuality education.[24]

Some cautions about language are important. Unfortunately, as in many areas of sexuality, language is inadequate here. The term *sexual orientation* is problematic because it suggests that there is some essential direction to one's sexuality, perhaps inborn. This has not been proven and is not likely to be (see Essentialism and the Search for the Origins of Homosexuality). *Sexual preference,* on the other hand, implies that one makes a simple choice or decision that can continually be redecided. This also is not the experience of most people. *Sexual identity* is the term I will use, since it avoids the question of "origins" and therefore the dilemmas of the first two terms. Its disadvantage is that it assumes the individual has, at least somewhat consciously, taken on the identity of heterosexual, lesbian, gay, or bisexual, and therefore it doesn't adequately address the large number of people who act in ways that are different from the category with which they identify. We know, for example, that many self-defined heterosexual men have sexual relationships with other men. Not inconsiderable numbers of lesbians and gay men have sex with partners of the other gender. In addition, some people shift their identities during their lives. Nevertheless, I will use the term sexual identity because, in this book on culture and sexuality, it is crucial to address questions of social categories and identities.

This imprecision of language highlights one of the central problems we face in trying to teach about lesbian and gay issues. That is, we, and therefore our curricula, often make assumptions about what it means to be lesbian or gay, and about the categories of homosexuality and heterosexuality, that are not supported by historical research. Specifically, instruction about homosexuality often reflects an essentialist point of view in which it is assumed that sexual categories mirror the reality of individuals' experiences (see Essentialism and the Search for the Origins of Homosexuality). We teach about homosexuality and heterosexuality as though such identities were "real" instead of categories that were made up a hundred years ago. In this section, then, in addition to examining how culture shapes and influences lesbian and gay identities, I will begin by addressing perhaps that most important aspect of the social construction of sexual identities: their invention in the nineteenth century.

The Invention of Sexual Identities

In February 1992, *Newsweek* ran a provocative cover featuring a close-up shot of a white, blue-eyed baby with the headline, "Is This Child Gay?" The inside story reported on the controversial research of Simon LeVay, who claimed to have discovered an area of the brain that causes homosexuality. The cover image was an important representation of our popular assumption that some people are gay and other people are heterosexual. This photo was meant to shock, however, in its suggestion that perhaps, even as children, such a distinction is present. It reinforced the idea that there are two fundamentally different kinds of sexual people: heterosexual and homosexual.

Notions of homosexual and heterosexual identity are only relatively recent—about one hundred years old. Before the late nineteenth century, there was no such thing as a homosexual person, or for that matter a heterosexual person. Individuals engaged in same-sex sexual activities, to be sure, but this did not mark them as "homosexuals." Sexual behavior, of any kind, was not central to one's social identity. This changed toward the end of the nineteenth century.

A number of factors in the late 1800s brought about the invention of sexual identities and the willingness to label people based on the gender of their sexual partner. Historians mark that as an era during which dominant sexual meanings shifted from an emphasis on family and reproduction to the sense that sexuality was vital to individual happiness and emotional intimacy.[25] This was, in part, because the demographic shift away from the rural household into the cities allowed individuals some independence from familial control over their sexuality. In the dominant culture, sexuality became increasingly personal, an important aspect of one's personality and a necessity for fulfillment. Before this change in sexual meaning it would have been unthinkable to categorize people based on sexual feelings and behaviors.

Another important factor in the invention of sexual identities was the growth in power of the legal and the medical professions. Although homosexual activity was subject to sodomy laws in England before 1885, historians emphasize that these laws were directed against specific *acts*, not particular *categories of people*.[26] Acts of sodomy committed between women and men were as vulnerable to prosecution as those between men and men. Laws passed beginning in 1885, however, began to target sexual acts between men. This coincided with the emergence of medical literature that defined same-sex sexual activity as an internal, individual trait.

Whereas earlier, then, religion and the law took note of *acts* of sodomy, the new medical and legal professions described a distinct kind of sexual *person*. A variety of terms for this new individual emerged beginning in the 1860s, including invert, urning, and homosexual. The year 1892 marks some of the earliest appearances of the word *homosexual* in medical texts. Homosexual, obviously, is the term that became most popular, although it has recently been displaced by *lesbian* and *gay* as a result of the lesbian and gay liberation movement. Soon after the invention of the category of homosexual, the term *heterosexual* began to appear in the literature. It was defined in various ways but eventually came to signify other-gender sexual attraction and activity.[27]

The idea that there were homosexual and heterosexual people was immediately adopted by most physicians and sexologists. Not everyone accepted such a proposition, however. Among modern sex researchers, the idea of stable sexual identities was most vehemently criticized by Alfred Kinsey. Unlike his predecessors, sexologists Krafft-Ebing and Havelock Ellis, who wrote about homosexuality as a congenital identity type, Kinsey refused to talk about homosexuality as an identity or even about homosexual persons. He believed everyone had the capacity for homosexuality, and so he spoke only of homosexual patterns of behavior. He noted that most males had some same-sex sexual experience during their lifetimes. He insisted that behavior is fluid and unstable, that the "world is not to be divided into sheep and goats. . . . Only the human mind invents categories and tries to force facts into separated pigeonholes."[28] Although he was one of the most influential sex researchers of the twentieth century, Kinsey's challenge to the idea of stable sexual identities went unheeded. Most sex researchers accept the terms without question.

One hundred years since their invention, we have lost the awareness that sexual identities are a product of our social world. The categories of homosexuality and heterosexuality seem simply to be a truth about our sexual universe; the idea that there are distinct heterosexual and homosexual persons forms the centerpiece of the sexual wisdom of our culture. We believe that this is simply the way people are. This assumption persists despite the failure of empirical research to support such a proposition and despite empirical (and anecdotal) data that would discourage such assumptions. People do not easily fit into sexual categories; they are not, as Kinsey warned us, sheep and goats. Our attempts to cram them into ill-fitting pigeonholes result in problems for educators.

The seemingly discrete boundaries of sexual identity have been directly challenged during the AIDS epidemic. AIDS educators, for example, have found their efforts complicated by their recognition that sexual behaviors and sexual identities do not always match. It is not unusual, for example, for Latino men who identify as heterosexual to engage in sexual activity with other men without this being a challenge to their straight identity.[29] And we know that it is not uncommon for European-American, self-identified heterosexual men to have sexual encounters with other men. This has prompted the educational use of cumbersome but more specific terms such as "men who have sex with men." A recent lesbian health survey showed that 14 percent of the women in the sample had had sexual contact with men within the two years of the survey.[30] There are few assumptions, it seems, that can be made about the sexual activities of individuals who identify as either heterosexual or homosexual.

Essentialism and the Search for the Origins of Homosexuality

Discoveries of a biological cause for homosexuality seem to fill the newspapers and airwaves these days. In just the last few years we've been told about the "gay brain," "gay genes," and "gay twins." The media show great enthusiasm for such findings, as do some gay activists, who erroneously believe that proof of biological causes will eliminate anti-gay discrimination. In fact, the search for biological origins of homosexuality is as old as the category itself, and so far it has been unsuccessful.

The belief that there is a biological basis for homosexuality reflects an essentialist perspective. It is based on the notion that there is an internal sex drive or instinct that comes from some anatomical or physiological source, such as hormones or brain structures. From this perspective, the type or direction of one's sexual interests—choosing same-sex partners, for example—is the result of such biological influences. The challenge has been to locate these influences.

This search is over one hundred years old. After they invented the categories, early physicians and sexologists hypothesized biological differences between homosexuals and heterosexuals. One explanation was that homosexuals were a "third sex"—that gay men had the brain of a woman in the body of a man. Implicit in this hypothesis is that the brain is the source of sexuality and desire. After the discovery of hormones in the early 1900s, some researchers suggested that homosexuals were hormonally unbalanced. Testosterone levels, they hypothesized, were inadequate in gay men.

So far, no biological theories hold up under rigorous research. Hormonal theories have consistently been disproved. There are no significant differences in hormone levels between heterosexuals and lesbians or gay men. Studies that have tried to "cure" gay men by injecting them with testosterone supplements had an unintended effect. The men reported an increased interest in sex, but they continued to direct that interest toward other men. The search for a hormonal cause has been largely abandoned.

Newer studies hypothesize structural sources of homosexuality, like the brain or genes. For example, researcher Simon LeVay in 1991 claimed to have found a section of the hypothalamus that differs for gay and heterosexual men. Although it received much attention, this study has been soundly criticized for problematic research methods. Many scientists believe that studies like LeVay's, which demonstrate a possible biological difference, are statistical flukes. Usually other researchers are unable to replicate these studies, and consistent replication is essential before scientists take the findings seriously.

Scientists have laid out a number of methodological criticisms of these types of findings. The sampling techniques are often problematic. For example, it is usually difficult, when working with corpses, to determine whether the person had been straight or gay when living (and what those self-identifications meant to the person and his behavior). LeVay assumed that, if not mentioned on the medical chart (most of his gay sample died of AIDS, another factor that might distort the findings), his subjects were heterosexual. Other potential problems include the way the brain section was sampled and measured, and the type of solution the tissues had been preserved in. Studies that claim a "gay gene" have also been criticized for sampling procedures and other methodological shortcomings.

It is likely that researchers will never discover a biological cause for homosexuality. Such efforts rest on the inaccurate assumption that these categories of sexual identity reflect real differences between people. But we know that sexuality is a continuum of feelings, attractions, and behaviors, and most people experience and behave in a range of different ways. Those who search for causes of heterosexuality and homosexuality are looking for the source of something that doesn't exist in nature but rather exists in our social world. As one scientist said, "It's like looking in the brain for your political party affiliation."[1]

The search will go on, for we live in a highly medicalized society in which scientists have led us to believe that biological causes can be found for almost any human behavior. And there is much enthusiasm for such a prospect—especially among the media, who glowingly report even the most shoddy research. We continually read that scientists have discovered the gene for alcoholism or the gene for gambling. Rarely do we see reports of the retractions when the studies cannot be replicated and are found to be inadequate.

Social constructionists have responded to these scientific efforts by trying to explain that sexuality is a more complicated domain that arises not from a biological drive but from a range of social, historical, and cultural influences. But this is a complicated argument, one that the media cannot easily fit into sound bites. Nevertheless, it is important to continue to challenge faulty research and distorted reporting that would lead people to the erroneous conclusion that our sexual identity is the result of our brains or genes.[2]

[1] Darrell Yates Rist, "Are Homosexuals Born That Way?" *The Nation,* October 19, 1992.

[2] Zella Luria and others, *Human Sexuality* (New York: Wiley, 1987); Gail Vines, *Raging Hormones: Do They Rule Our Lives?* (Berkeley: University of California Press, 1994).

. . . .

What are the implications of the invention of sexual identities for sexuality educators? Should the categories of heterosexuality, lesbian, and gay be thrown out? How can we teach about sexual differences without using these terms? These questions speak to the difficulties of bringing a historical and cultural approach to sexuality education. But such an approach, while perhaps complicated, allows our programs to be more accurate and effective.

There are two major arenas in which we can integrate the awareness that sexual identities are unstable and invented categories. First, this insight will alter how we approach our audiences. Sexuality educators have made the important shift to the recognition that not all students are heterosexual. The next important shift is gaining an awareness that while students may identify themselves as either heterosexual or lesbian or gay, their behaviors may well fall outside the borders of these identities. This is especially true for adolescents. One study of adolescent lesbians in New York City found that three-quarters of them were engaging in sexual intercourse with males and that they reported more male sexual partners than national samples of female adolescents.[31] Categories of sexual identity are fluid, and people may move in and out of them or even define them in different ways.

The second important arena for change is how we teach about sexual identities. Most curricula are built on the assumption that the categories of heterosexuality and homosexuality are stable and real. Some even suggest that people are born with a fixed sexual orientation. Such curricula are well intentioned. They raise consciousness and teach tolerance and acceptance of sexual difference. These are crucial and difficult goals in a homophobic society. Unfortunately, this approach reinforces the inaccurate idea that there are discrete sexual categories. It assumes that there are different kinds of people, straight and lesbian or gay, who inhabit different worlds and behave in different ways. As we have seen, this isn't necessarily so, and it is problematic to continue to teach students that it is.

How, then, do we approach this dilemma? How can we teach students to accept and value sexual difference while teaching them that heterosexuality and homosexuality, as rigid types, don't exist? This poses a seemingly unsolvable problem, one with which social theorists have been addressing concerning not just sexual identity but also categories such as race and gender. The solution entails opening up our ideas about culture and sexuality as well as about curricula and teaching strategies.

Even though we recognize that sexual identities are invented categories that can be unstable, we cannot simply dismiss their relevance or importance. The categories of heterosexuality and homosexuality have existed for one hundred years, and our sex/gender system has been constructed around them. Further, one group, that of lesbians and gay men, has been the target of prejudice and discrimination. We must focus on that social fact and seek to correct it, even though to do so almost implicitly reinforces the idea that such categories have some tangible reality.

The alternative perspective is one discussed in Chapter Two in relation to dilemmas posed by the social construction of cultures. We would approach sexual identities as "necessary fictions."[32] By "fiction" we mean that these are invented categories that often don't really tell us much about a person's behaviors, beliefs, or values. On the other hand, sexual identities are "necessary" because we need them in our daily lives. Because the categories of heterosexual, lesbian, gay, and bisexual already exist, we can no more refuse to locate ourselves in one of them than we can ignore the categories of gender or race. If we do ignore them we marginalize ourselves in relation to a social group (just as if we refused a racial identification we could not organize with others who made the identification). Also, by ignoring sexual identification we reinforce the invisibility of lesbians and gay men.

There are sound educational reasons to teach students that sexual identities have been invented, that they are "necessary fictions." It is no more complicated than teaching them other historical lessons. The advantage of revising the curriculum in such a fashion is that we can begin to alter some of the inaccurate and destructive thinking about sexual identities in order to more accurately speak to students' experiences. We can stop teaching that there are "sheep and goats" in our sexual world and help them recognize that there is a range and complexity to human sexual behavior.

Culture and Homophobia

Although all sexual identities are recent inventions, heterosexuality is, of course, the privileged social norm. Homophobia—the fear and hatred of lesbians and gay men—serves as a mechanism to regulate sexuality, to push people in the direction of a heterosexual identification. But homophobia is not a stable social force. It is a set of beliefs, values, and behaviors concerning heterosexuality and homosexuality that can change over time and across cultural groups. It is important, when working with diverse groups, to recognize that anti-gay feelings and behaviors may take different forms among different people.

When we say that history and culture shape the nature of homophobia we mean that the background and traditions of a group give a specific set of meanings to anti-gay sentiment. One clear example of this is homophobia in the black community. It is important to remember that homophobia exists, in some fashion and degree, in every culture and community. So to single out the black community to illustrate the cultural construction of homophobia is not to suggest that it is necessarily more homophobic on some objective scale. But it serves as a good example because national data indicate greater disapproval of homosexuality by blacks compared to whites.[33] And, as Harlan Dalton suggests, the black community differs from the larger society in its denunciation of homosexuality, in that "our verbal attacks seem tinged with cruelty and are usually delivered with an offhandedness that many White observers find unnerving."[34]

We can understand this dynamic through cultural analysis. This is not to suggest that there is something inherent in blacks as individuals or a culture that fuels homophobia. Rather, there are social, historical, and cultural factors specific to the black community's relationship to the dominant society that help explain its distinctive patterns of hostility to homosexuality.

In this example we see again the importance of a group's social-structural position in shaping certain cultural traditions. Slavery and the ongoing consequences of racism have left African Americans in a weakened economic and political position, with less access to well-paying jobs and careers, good housing, comprehensive health care, and equal educational opportunities. Family life was often fragmented. Cultural patterns that arose in response to these conditions have proven fertile ground for the growth of anti-gay perspectives.

A strong black church, which has been a traditional source of both support and liberation work, and an emphasis on religion are factors that shape homophobia.[35] Many black churches adhere to fundamentalist Christian doctrines in which homosexuality is prohibited. Such teaching casts homosexuality as deviant, sinful, and immoral behavior that will be punished by God. Religion, then, which has been a source of solace for many African Americans, may encourage anti-gay sentiment.

Concern about the black family is a major factor underlying homophobia among African Americans. As Dalton notes, slavery exerted an enormously destructive influence on families and the relationships between black men and women. One lingering consequence is an emphasis on conventional gender roles, in particular strong "masculine" men. Homosexuality is seen as a threat to the intact black family; "openly gay men and lesbians evoke hostility in part because they have come to symbolize the strong female and the weak male that slavery and Jim Crow produced."[36] From this perspective, the meaning of homophobia among blacks is more about gender roles than about sexuality.

As we have noted, however, homophobia is a complex set of beliefs and activities. And, as bell hooks and Dalton point out, there are contradictions in the practice of homophobia by blacks; "a cruel tongue is often used to hide a tender heart."[37] Blacks have a long tradition of verbal aggression and accusation—"playing the dozens." But this practice, when directed at lesbians and gay men, does not always translate into direct action. There can be a chasm between what people say and what they do. So despite homophobia, the black community often embraces black lesbians and gay men (although, as Dalton notes, not without lesbians and gay men paying a price).

One can, undoubtedly, trace the roots of homophobia to particular social and historical influences within specific cultural groups. Because of different historical experiences and social locations, those influences will vary, so that, for example, the specifics among Asian Americans will be different than among African Americans or Anglo Americans. In order to combat homophobia, it is useful to understand its particular origins and how those factors may differ across cultures.

Lesbian and Gay Cultures

There is not one way to be lesbian or gay. The range of experiences is wide, shaped by cultural factors. To acknowledge this diversity, a 1978 study from the Institute for Sex Research (informally known as the Kinsey Institute) was entitled *Homosexualities*. The authors stressed that "there is no such thing as *the* homosexual (or *the* heterosexual, for that matter)" (emphasis in original).[38] Different cultures influence how one is heterosexual, lesbian, or gay in highly variable ways. This diversity has important implications for the types of programs sexuality educators develop.

A range of factors, such as race and ethnicity, gender, social class, and age, influence the sets of meanings and symbols attached to being lesbian or gay. Further, these differences cross-cut, so that individuals have multiple identifications in which sexual scripts conflict. One striking example of this is the difficulty experienced by lesbians and gay men of color, who can often find themselves torn between their racial culture and their sexual identity. Gloria Anzaldúa, for example, has written eloquently about being on the "borderlands," the margin between her Chicana cultural background (itself a meeting of two cultures) and the lesbian and gay community.[39]

Cultural traditions and practices infuse the experience of being lesbian or gay in various ways. For example, a strong family structure and rigid gender roles shape lesbian and gay identity for Chicanos. Although family regulation of sexuality has loosened throughout this century among the white middle class, allowing individuals more sexual autonomy, this process has not occurred to a comparable degree among Latinos and Chicanos.[40] Many lesbians and gay men from these groups experience enormous difficulty coming out, for they risk rejection by the family, a group that has served as some protection against racism.

A closely knit family structure can affect sexuality in many ways. Chicanos may be unable to stay out at night socializing, move out of the home, or move in with a male lover.[41] Moraga writes that she risked being labeled a traitor or sellout by seeking sexual independence through her participation in dominant, white culture. It is the accusation that "hangs above the heads and beats in the hearts of most Chicanas, seeking to develop our own autonomous sense of ourselves, particularly our sexuality."[42]

Rigid gender roles also shape Chicano homosexuality. Almaguer describes how ideas about power and dominance, particularly as they relate to masculinity and femininity, permeate the meanings of homosexual behavior among Mexican and Mexican-American men.[43] Unlike among European Americans, for whom gender of sexual partner is the defining aspect of homosexuality, the "Mexican/Latin-American sexual system . . . confers meaning to homosexual practices according to sexual aim—i.e. the act one wants to perform with another person (of either biological sex)."[44] In Latin culture, the gay male sexual universe is divided into the one who penetrates and the partner who is penetrated. The insertive partner is considered masculine and may well identify himself as heterosexual. He can even gain status among his peers for a large number of male conquests.

On the other hand, the receptive partner is seen as stigmatized, submissive, and feminized. He is not a man. Chicano men in the U.S. may often retain the dynamics of this sexual system, weaving them together with certain sexual cultural practices of European-American gay males.

The strong patriarchal system among Chicanos can shape lesbian sexual identity as well. Moraga described how her struggle to forge an autonomous sexuality as a lesbian gave rise to enormous conflicts about her role as a woman in the family, her identification with and love for her mother, and her religious teachings about what it meant to be a good woman.[45] She eventually defined herself as a "butch" lesbian, a move that Almaguer notes was likely an expression of the rigid gender-coded sexuality Moraga learned in her family.

What it means to be sexual, for heterosexuals as well as lesbians and gay men, evolves and changes. The process of self-definition, the relationship to the family, one's choice of partner, and one's preference for certain sexual activities are all aspects of sexual identities that are variable. They are constructed by social, cultural, and historical influences. There is no universal formula. Instead, there are a range of practices that are specific to particular cultural groups.

Culture, Gender, and Sexuality

There is a memorable scene in the movie *Annie Hall* where Annie (played by Diane Keaton) and Alvy Singer (played by Woody Allen) are visiting their separate therapists. Each therapist asks how often they have sex. Annie and Alvy both agree on the number of times a week—three—but they differ wildly in how they characterize the amount of their lovemaking. Annie describes it as constant, and Alvy describes it as almost nonexistent. This exchange has been repeated often, as it apparently struck a collective cultural nerve about stereotypical differences in male and female sexuality.

The *Annie Hall* scene is rich in implications for sexuality educators. In fact, it highlights one of the central social constructionist themes of this book: that the same sexual event or activity can be experienced differently and hold very different meanings for people in different cultural groups. While there is some debate among feminist scholars about whether gender can be appropriately considered a culture, there is no disagreement that gender constitutes a social category that can profoundly influence lives in countless ways.[1] Gender can shape us in structural and economic ways—for example, determining access to certain types of jobs and influencing our salary. And gender can govern our psychological and emotional worlds, determining our feelings about sexuality.

The nature of the connection between gender and sexuality is crucial for sexuality educators, who often work with coed audiences. Loosely speaking, such a group can be considered multicultural based on gender differences. Educators can safely assume that, due to different social locations, the men and women in the audience may well bring different interpretations and sets of background experiences to the classroom. But what exactly are these different experiences and interpretations? How does gender shape sexuality, and vice versa? What assumptions, if any, can sexuality educators make about female and male sexuality? As with all the questions about culture and sexuality we've discussed, the answers are far from simple and obvious.

There is a popular cultural narrative about gender and sexuality that is powerful and pervasive. In this cultural scenario, men are sexually aggressive and insatiable. They are always on the lookout for sex, ready to engage at a moment's notice. In this script, male sexuality is virtually synonymous with and centered around the penis. And penises, as Bernie Zilbergeld writes in his chapter "It's Two Feet Long, Hard as Steel, and Can Go All Night, and Will Knock Your Socks Off," always come in three sizes: "large, gigantic, and so big you can barely get them through the doorway."[2]

Women, on the reverse side of this cultural picture, are sexually timid. Their sexuality is pure and quiet and needs coaxing. This is the "madonna" script. Women's sexuality is supposedly not genitally oriented and is often represented in films and novels by diffuse images like walking on the beach or peeling and eating an orange. There is also, of course, that other category of women: the "whore." These are presumably the ones with whom the insatiable men, with their battering-ram penises, are feverishly copulating. This distinction among women holds across many cultural groups. Among Asian-American women, for example, there are the stereotypes of the passive, subservient woman and the strong, overly aggressive "dragon lady."[3] Hispanic men in California described two types of women: the "girl next door," and bad girls, the "daughters of the night."[4]

Although I've sketched these cultural stereotypes here as near-caricatures, it would be a mistake to dismiss their continuing influence. Some of the most publicized cultural events of the 1990s have underscored these sex/gender stereotypes. The rape trials of Mike Tyson and William Kennedy Smith circulated familiar ideas about the female tease and the man who couldn't stop once aroused. And the Anita Hill–Clarence Thomas hearings showed how quickly a dignified and respectable woman could have her image transformed into that of the spurned, vengeful "whore."[5] Male and female sexual scripts continue to reflect a double standard in terms of responsibility, accountability, and experience.

There is another popular cultural scenario about gender and sexuality. In this script, women aren't really interested in sex; instead they want relationships. Sex is merely the chip they bargain with in order to attain intimacy and connection. Or in a related version, women don't want sex—they want to hug and snuggle. This was dramatically publicized by the results of a 1984 Ann Landers column in which she polled her women readers with the question, "Would you be content to be held close and treated tenderly and forget about 'the act'?" Over 90,000 women responded, with 72 percent choosing the snuggle over "the act." In this version of the script, of course, men play out their aggressive and insatiable interest in "the act," using false promises of love, relationships, marriage, and anything else in order to achieve it. The *Newsweek* columnist who reported on the Ann Landers column summed up this sex/gender script as that of "an America in which silently suffering women are exploited by selfish and frequently foul-smelling men."[6]

Sexuality education often reinforces the notion of different male and female sexual scripts. Texts and other materials typically describe male sexuality as active and potentially uncontrollable, with female sexuality weaker and more muted. This often translates into women being responsible for controlling the level of sexual behavior, since they are supposedly more able to stop. It is she who must be responsible for birth control, safer sex, and determining "how far to go." Using outdated and often discredited information on hormones, the brain, and genes, these lessons reinforce essentialist ideas about sexuality, "sex drive," and gender.[7]

Scholarship of the last twenty-five years has questioned the role of biology in gender differences. This literature is so vast that even a short review is well beyond the scope of this book. However, it reveals no conclusive evidence that hormones, brain structures or functions, genetic patterns, or any other physiological influences determine male and female differences such as those sometimes seen regarding sexuality.[8] The notion that our sexuality and gender are biologically determined has been repeatedly challenged; critics suggest that the belief hurts both women and men by keeping them in rigid roles and wrongfully suggesting that their life options are limited.

If we reject these problematic essentialist ideas about gender and sex, what are we left with? No one would deny that men and women sometimes exhibit strikingly different patterns of behavior. So how do we explain them? Scholars have engaged in the same debates about essentialism and social constructionism with regard to gender as they have concerning sexuality (see Chapter One). Most agree on a social constructionist explanation of gender differences—that is, that biology does not determine behavior. As some scholars have quipped, there are no genes that determine interest and ability in cooking or mechanics.

Further, gender is a historically changing social category. For example, what it meant to be a man and what it meant to be a woman were different in 1890 than they were in 1990. In addition—and this is crucial for our purposes—gender categories are shaped by such other cultural categories as race and ethnicity. So ideas about maleness and femaleness can vary among African Americans, Latinos, whites, and Asian Americans. Gender categories are fluid, unstable, and given meaning based on particular social, cultural, economic, and political influences.

It is clear, then, that making generalizations about gender and sexuality is difficult. We must clearly specify that any perceived differences are social and cultural in origin, not biological. For example, the fact that men generally engage in intercourse earlier than women is related to social factors that include greater cultural permission and encouragement. It is not because young men are being driven by hormonal forces they can't control. In her research on white, working-class couples, Lillian Rubin pointed out that men's focus on sex and women's emphasis on emotional relationships have cultural origins. These responses reflect a socialization process in which women are encouraged in all areas of personality development except that of sexual expression while men are constricted in all areas of emotional development save that of the sexual realm.[9]

Generalizations about gender and sexuality must indicate which groups of men and women are being considered. As we saw in Chapter Four, sexual behaviors and patterns can vary by culture. So, too, may the ways in which gender shapes sexuality vary by culture. For example, the ways in which Asian-American males experience and pattern their sexuality can look very different from those of African-American men.

There are several aspects of the relationship between gender and sexuality that are of importance to sexuality educators as they design and implement programs. I have loosely divided these into three categories: sexual behaviors, sexual experiences and meanings, and relationship dynamics.

Sexual Behaviors

Most research does show differences between men and women in patterns of sexual behaviors. Across several different categories of race and ethnicity, men tend to have sexual intercourse at an earlier age than women. The National Longitudinal Survey of Youth clearly revealed these differences.[10] At the age of fifteen, 12 percent of white boys had had intercourse compared to 5 percent of girls. Among African Americans at age fifteen, 42 percent of boys compared to 10 percent of girls had had intercourse; 19 percent of Hispanic boys compared to 4 percent of Hispanic girls had had first coitus by age fifteen. Lesbian adolescents tend to "come out" at a later age than gay male adolescents.[11] When sexuality educators address a group of young adolescents, then, many more of the boys in the audience have had intercourse or a gay sexual experience than girls.

Differences in sexual behavior by gender show up among adults as well. Alfred Kinsey carefully documented differences among whites in his famous survey research published in 1948 and 1953.[12] Most of the differences can be quickly summarized as fewer women engaging in fewer behaviors less often than men. For example, he found that by age forty-five, 33 percent of women as compared to 83 percent of men had had nocturnal sex dreams to orgasm. By the age of twenty, 33 percent of women had masturbated to orgasm compared to 92 percent of men. And by age forty, 26 percent of women and 50 percent of men had had extramarital affairs.

It is important to remember that the Kinsey data is old, and some of the men and women he interviewed were born in the late nineteenth century. Clearly, sexual politics have changed, as have the norms and expectations of our sex/gender system. These changes clearly affect sexual behavior, and some of the differences reported by Kinsey are not quite so pronounced today. But one striking aspect of the Kinsey data is that, despite a more restrictive set of sex/gender norms in the first half of the century, such a large number of women reported engaging in such behaviors as masturbation and adultery. It is certainly noteworthy that more than one-quarter of women in the first half of this century reported extramarital affairs. Kinsey's book on female sexuality caused an enormous scandal when it was published in 1953, for his findings belied the stereotype of the passive, sexually uninterested woman.[13]

In an examination of several data sources between 1938 and 1970, sociologists Weinberg and Williams showed sexual differences between both black and white women and men.[14] For example, one data set showed that 28.7 percent of black men compared to 3.1 percent of black women had engaged in coitus by age fifteen. Only 28.7 percent of black women reported any extramarital petting or coitus compared to 76.1 percent of men. Among whites, 7 percent of women said they think about sex quite a bit, compared to 59 percent of men.

The National Health and Social Life Survey, published in 1994, revealed similar patterns.[15] In the category of masturbation, among a total sample of more than 3,000 respondents, 36.7 percent of men compared to 58.3 percent of women said they had never masturbated. Other patterns emerge when the findings are broken down by race and ethnicity. There are comparable gender differences among whites and Hispanics: 33.4 percent of white men compared to 55.7 percent of white women and 33.1 percent of Hispanic men compared to 65.5 percent of Hispanic women claimed no history of masturbation. There was virtually no gender difference among blacks, although their overall figures are the highest of all racial or ethnic groups except for Hispanic women: 60.3 percent of black men compared to 67.8 percent of black women said they had never masturbated. The NHSLS is important because it is the most recent, comprehensive sex survey to show how social factors such as gender and race or ethnicity interact to organize sexual behavior.

Centuries of laws, regulations, norms, expectations, and values help explain the different behavior patterns between women and men. Men, unlike women, have been given social permission to be sexual. Indeed, they are expected to be sexual. And unlike girls, boys may feel few limits on their sexual behavior. In a longitudinal study of family communication patterns about sexuality, Kahn found that among families where parents claimed that they had set rules about dating and sexuality, 60 percent of the boys and 36 percent of the girls reported that there were no rules.[16] Girls whose parents set more rules scored lower on a scale of sexual comfort than girls without rules. For boys, there was no apparent impact of rules, one obvious reason being that mostly they didn't think the rules were set for them. This is a striking example of the different sexual worlds of men and women, of the ways in which interpretations and meanings differ, and of how those differences may shape sexual behavior.

Sexual Experiences and Meanings

In addition to what they actually do, men and women may often be different in how they experience sexuality and in the meanings they attach to sex. As we discussed earlier, one familiar cultural script is that men want sex and not relationships while women, who really only want relationships, will trade sex for love. This narrative drives countless novels, movies, and television shows. It forms the basis of the traditional double standard. When the roles are reversed, as in the book *Looking for Mr. Goodbar*, the woman pays a steep price.

How accurately does this script reflect the sexual meaning systems of men and women? What evidence do we have, other than that from television and 90,000 Ann Landers readers? If we look to social science and history, which can often simply reflect and reinforce themes from the dominant culture, we can get some hints about how widely this generalization holds.

Some researchers argue that these patterns emerge as early as adolescence, a time when young women and men are just becoming sexual. Certainly, one rarely spoken assumption in sexuality education materials for youth is that the boy will try to get as much as he can from the vulnerable and smitten girl. It is worth an in-depth look at two sophisticated studies on adolescent sexuality for the different views they provide on male-female dynamics.

Adolescent sexuality can effectively be analyzed only in a broader social and political context. Sociologist Elijah Anderson views the sex codes of youth in the poor, black neighborhood of Northton as the cultural manifestation of urban poverty, a response to deprivation and limited opportunity.[17] From this perspective, sex is not the product of teens' drives and instincts but rather a domain of values and activities whose meanings reflect and in turn act on the surrounding society and culture.

Anderson's depiction of Northton's sex/gender system reinforces the prevailing cultural narrative of gender differences. Sex in Northton is a battleground where young men and women stake out what it means to be male or female. To the boy, sex represents status among his peers. His goal, then, is to get as much sex as possible, since "the more 'pussy' he gets, the more esteem accrues to him."[18] According to Anderson, the girls, predictably, long for love, relationships, commitment, and a family. These opposing visions result in sex being a contest where boys and girls each try to succeed at their goals. The results are often disappointing for both.

Anderson dubs the different male and female sexual scripts among Northton's youth "the game and the dream." It is no surprise that the boy's script is the game. Young men, according to Anderson, mount campaigns for "getting over" a girl's sexual defenses. His game is reflected in all the ways in which he presents himself to her: his dress, dancing ability, and conversation. One young man said about the game: "They trickin' them good. Either the woman is trickin' the man, or the man is trickin' the woman. Good! They got a trick. She's thinkin' it's [the relationship] one thing, he playin' another game, you know. He thinkin' she alright, and she doing something else."[19] Part of the boys' game is to pretend the love and commitment the girl allegedly desires.

Girls' dreams are fueled by both the deprivation and poverty in their lives and the images of love and family that surround them in popular songs and television. They want stability and a future. But girls are not stupid. They see all around them that boys lied to girls and left them pregnant and alone. One girl told Anderson: "Yeah, they'll [boys will] take you out. Walk you down to Center City, movies, window shop [laughs]. They point in the window, 'Yeah, I'm gonna get this. Wouldn't you like this? Look at that nice livin' room set.' Then they want to take you to his house, go to his room: 'Let's go over to my house, watch some TV.' Next thing you know your clothes is off and you in bed havin' sex, you know."[20]

Anderson's portrait of Northton's sexual battlefield supports the cultural narrative that men want sex and women want love. He points out that women are not simply passive victims but rather strong women who fight, albeit unsuccessfully, for what they want.

Yet we are left with a striking picture of gender stereotypes in the world he depicts.

What Anderson doesn't show us is any rebellion or resistance on the part of the girls. He shows their unwavering commitment to a gender-based dream of love and marriage. But is this the dream of all young women? If so, what are we to make of some of the emerging voices of girls who say otherwise, such as rap singers Queen Latifah, Yo-Yo, and Salt-N-Pepa? Might not some girls also have a "game"?

Researcher Sharon Thompson identifies such girls from a comprehensive nationwide study of adolescent girls' sexuality. She calls these girls "the tricksters."[21] Compared to the boys, not many girls become tricksters. Thompson details the obstacles facing many of the girls she interviewed: African-American teenagers living in poverty, without much education, from unstable homes, facing uncertain but certainly limited futures. And yet despite this, or perhaps because of it, a group of girls take the boys' game and turn it inside out.

. . . .

Rap Music and Black Women's Sexuality

Tricksters probably listen to rap. Rap music examines many of the dynamics in young, black, heterosexual relationships. Rap music is, as critic Tricia Rose points out, a form of public discussion about contemporary life in the black urban working class. Black women have been writing rap music with an emphasis, as the lyrics and videos of women rappers reveal, on the complexities of black women's sexuality.

Rap music has been the subject of much controversy and has been criticized for glorifying violence and promoting sexism. In her book, *Black Noise: Rap Music and Black Culture in Contemporary America,* Rose points out that rap is a contradictory cultural form that sends out diverse messages.[1] Not all male rappers are sexist (nor are all women rappers antisexist). When we listen more closely to rap we hear this complexity.

Gender relations and sexuality are important themes in rap. Artists like Salt-N-Pepa and MC Lyte celebrate black women as strong, savvy, and sexually powerful. Many raps comment on the male "game," as discussed by Elijah Anderson (see "Sexual Experiences and Meanings"). These raps depict women as subverting this game, since they are too wise to fall for the false promises of men. Some show women turning the tables on men, tricking men for their own advantage, as in Icey Jaye's "It's a Girl Thang," in which women lavishly spend their dates' money while they laugh at men whom they fool. We can see how rap is an important cultural expression that foregrounds women's sexuality, independence, and resistance to traditional gender relations.

Rap music is an important domain for sexuality educators. It is a popular and vital form of cultural expression for young, urban African Americans. The centrality of themes about sexuality and heterosexual relationships show this to be an area of great concern for young people. Rap music both teaches them sexual messages and reflects their sexual worlds. Rap can help us glimpse a part of this world.

[1] Tricia Rose, *Black Noise: Rap Music and Black Culture in Contemporary America* (Hanover, N. H.: Wesleyan University Press, 1994).

. . . .

Thompson's narrators have given up on the dream. They embrace sex for what it offers and for what they can wring out of it: pleasure, adventure, revenge. They are cold and nasty, refusing the scam of the boys' games. As Thompson says about them, "To be cold to love is proof against emotional and erotic blackmail. When these narrators say they can 'take or leave sex' or 'your romance doesn't phase me,' they position themselves beyond male persuasions. In a state of romantic alienation, they won't take shit, and they cannot be talked into buying or selling love."[22]

Thompson doesn't pretend that these girls have found a satisfying and effective alternative to the dream. Rather, the trickster's posture is a coping defense. Yet ultimately it is no more defensive or prone to disillusionment than either the girls' dream or the boys' game described by Anderson. Both Thompson and Anderson acknowledge that these adolescents need more than healthier emotional positions. For their lives to really change, so too must economic, racial, and gender-related inequality.

The figure of the female trickster is important because she introduces complexity into our cultural stories. She reminds us that individuals can fashion interpersonal scripts that are different from cultural scenarios. Cultures do not simply determine our behavior but serve as guides. The trickster shows us that cultural expectations have had an impact but that girls are capable of rebelling in order to fashion their own strategies of resistance and visions of a different future. So while it is evident that men and women often attach different meanings to sex, it is not always simple to determine what those meanings are and whether particular individuals or groups hold to dominant cultural narratives.

The awareness that women and men may have different ways of experiencing and attributing meaning to sexuality has proven of use to sexuality educators. For example, a very popular AIDS education program for gay men is the "house party." In Boston this type of program is called Safety Net; in New York it is called Hot, Horny, and Healthy. Each session is held in a man's home with a small group of friends or acquaintances. They provide HIV/AIDS information in the context of making safer sex "hot and horny." There is much explicit discussion and joking. The men participate in exercises where they fantasize "healthy" sexual activities that can be performed with different body parts. They work in small groups to develop a group safer-sex fantasy. These programs have been enormously successful in helping to transform cultural scenarios in the gay male community to be more supportive of condom use and other safer-sex practices.

When it became clear that women were getting HIV/AIDS, some educators sought to adapt the Safety Net model for use with women. It was immediately clear to most women's AIDS educators that the program would need to be radically changed in order to work for women. Most heterosexual women, especially those from Haitian and Latino cultures where sexuality is often less explicitly discussed, do not have the comfort with sexuality that gay men do. They have not had the level of sexual permission afforded to men by our society. And in particular, they are often not at ease with their bodies. Program developers were able to use information about some of the ways in which women's sexual universes are different in order to adjust the program to be more relevant for women.

It is difficult to imagine an AIDS education program for women entitled "Hot, Horny, and Healthy." Horniness, which connotes a powerful, sexual hunger, is a feeling supposedly only for men. A dominant European-American cultural scenario, one supported by centuries of religious doctrine, medical literature, and popular narratives (such as Ann Landers' column), is that women do not feel desire. And if they do it is immoral, unhealthy, unfeminine, or undignified. As with other cultural scenarios, however, this script about women's lack of desire has had an impact, but women have also crafted other experiences of sexual passion and adventure.

Cultural scenarios about women's sexual desire have varied throughout U.S. history. Historians point out that the medical literature painted two opposing portraits of women's sexuality in the nineteenth century. In one, women were depicted as strongly passionate; in the other they were seen as approaching sex "with shrinking, or even with horror, rather than with desire."[23] The nineteenth-century idea of women's passionlessness marked a departure from eighteenth-century ideas that women were lustful creatures prone to sexual excess.[24] These changes in ideas about whether women are either lustful or frigid rest not on the actual experiences of women but on broader social belief systems about sexuality and gender.

As the twentieth century comes to a close, our culture has grown increasingly accepting of women's passion.[25] The 1960s and 1970s marked a significant turning point in terms of attitudes. The glut of media information about women's sexuality during that time reflected both a growing openness and increasing sexological expertise. Many women were empowered not merely to avoid exploitive sex but to seek out fantasy, orgasms, and thrills. Feminist consciousness-raising groups helped women criticize problems in their existing sexual relationships and led them to exploration of new sexual terrain. A study of married couples in the early 1970s revealed greater sexual experimentation among white couples of all classes. Mainstream books like *The Joy of Sex*, *The Sensuous Woman*, and *My Secret Garden* spoke to a new sexual spirit. By the late 1970s, women had become increasingly active partners, and couples were enthusiastically proclaiming the importance of sex for a good relationship. One sign that women's desire has become more acceptable is that their lack of it is now considered a sexual dysfunction: inhibited sexual desire.[26]

If cultural scripts about women's desire are changing, what does this mean about women's actual experiences? As usual, it is difficult to say in the absence of good research. Many sex researchers have either assumed girls do not experience desire or have overlooked the subject entirely. This has resulted in what psychologist Michelle Fine calls "the missing discourse of desire" in sexuality education programs.[27]

We know, however, that women and girls do experience sexual passion. Women's diaries from the eighteenth and nineteenth centuries show often intense interest in sex.[28] Books, movies, songs, and other sources throughout this century reveal desire among women. And certainly contemporary popular magazines sell countless issues by tapping into women's sexual interest. Thompson's female trickster, as well as other girls she interviewed, expressed sexual curiosity, desire, and adventure. Fine discovered that, although no one else was talking about girls' desire, they themselves were talking about it. And psychologist Deborah Tolman interviewed groups of black and white girls who were quite willing to talk about their sexual desire.[29]

Lesbians face competing sets of expectations concerning sexual desire. One the one hand, they are women and therefore subject to the belief system that they are less interested in sex than men. On the other hand, they are lesbians and therefore part of an identity group that has been defined by sexuality and often viewed as hyper-sexual. As Raymond notes, "If the opposition of the male and the female is at bottom the opposition of desire and non-desire, then the lesbian adolescent represents the absence of desire; on the other hand, as sexual outlaw, she becomes *pure desire*, out of control and forfeiting the 'protections' afforded by traditional femininity" (emphasis in original).[30] We don't have a great deal of data, but it appears that lesbians may respond much more to their socialization as women in that couples seeking therapy report lack of desire more than any other sexual complaint.[31]

Sexual violence against women has been a significant obstacle to women's experience of their sexual passion and to their willingness to acknowledge and discuss it. As both children and adults, women have been subjected to both threats and the reality of abuse, from rape and incest to sexual harassment. Sexual violence is one major manifestation of male dominance over women. The reality of abuse, as well as women's legitimate fears of violence, police women's sexuality and result in the tension for women between "pleasure and danger."[32] As anthropologist Carole Vance notes, a range of influences from violence to cultural prohibitions work to diminish women's passion. "As a result, female desire is suspect from its first tingle, questionable until proven safe, and frequently too expensive when evaluated within the larger cultural framework which poses the question: is it really worth it? When unwanted pregnancy, street harassment, stigma, unemployment, queer-bashing, rape, and arrest are arrayed on the side of caution and inaction, passion often doesn't have a chance."[33]

This pleasure/danger split is one that most heterosexual men do not experience. This constitutes one of the most significant differences in the sexual meaning systems between men and women. It illustrates how male power has a tangible impact on women's sexuality. Even if a woman has not been personally abused, the fear exerts a widespread effect. The issue of power arises in our discussion of gender with regard not only to sexual experiences and meanings but also to relationship dynamics.

Relationship Dynamics

Among the many complicated dynamics to be negotiated in a relationship, heterosexual couples face the added complexity of gender differences and inequality. In addition to potential cultural differences in how men and women approach the world, there are also profound structural differences. Gender inequality is structurally embedded in our social world. Male dominance is exerted in diverse areas, from political life, where women candidates still face an uphill battle, to the workplace, where men—especially white men—typically earn more than women for comparable jobs, to the bedroom, where men and women may seem to inhabit different sexual universes. Not surprisingly, struggles over power and control often infuse the sexual relationships of heterosexual couples across race, ethnicity, and socioeconomic class.[34] It is important to point out that lesbian and gay relationships, as well as heterosexual ones, are affected by the interaction of gender and sexuality. Unlike heterosexuals, they don't have to deal with issues that might arise out of gender inequality, but there may be certain dynamics that come up when a couple is composed of two women or two men.

It is within relationships—heterosexual, lesbian, or gay—that such issues as pleasure and safety are negotiated, making this an arena of particular importance for sexuality and AIDS educators. The success or failure of contraception or safer sex depends on what happens between individual men and women whose worldviews have been shaped by a range of social, cultural, economic, and political influences. One issue of particular importance is the question of power: how power operates in relationships and which partner is more or less powerful.

The importance and impact of gender inequality and male power and dominance cannot be overemphasized in the field of sexuality education. Sexologists have a history of addressing such sexual issues as contraception—or such sexual problems as impotence or inability of women to have orgasms—as though men and women are complete equals in a relationship.[35] Only recently have they begun to acknowledge and address the ways in which males may dominate and control diverse aspects of a relationship, including sexuality. Men may control what gets talked about, if anything, between the couple. They may decide which sexual activities should take place and when. This level of control is possible because relationships operate in a broader context of male social and sexual dominance.

Having emphasized male power and dominance, it is also important to point out the complexities of the question of power. Power is not an all-or-nothing force that someone either has or does not have; it is a set of dynamics that operates in diffuse and complicated ways. It is inaccurate, therefore, to say that men have power in the heterosexual sexual relationship and women do not. It is necessary to try to discover specifically how power operates among men and women in relationships and how these dynamics might vary based on such factors as socioeconomic class, race, and ethnicity.

Gender differences that affect power dynamics spring not from biological differences between women and men, or even simply from different socialization. They arise from diverse social, political, and economic influences. A useful example of this, because of its stark dimensions, is machismo, an allegedly strong source of gender polarization in various Latino and Chicano groups. The traditional literature paints a familiar, if grim, portrait of gender among Chicanos. As Michael Miller points out, "Sex roles are rigidly dichotomized with the male conforming to the dominant-aggressive archetype, and the female being the polar opposite—subordinate and passive. The father is the unquestioned patriarch—the family provider, protector and judge. His word is law and demands strict obedience. Presumably, he is perpetually obsessed with the need to prove his manhood, oftentimes through excessive drinking, fighting, and/or extramarital conquests."[36]

There are two questions to consider about this picture. First, how do we explain these differences? And second, is this depiction still accurate?

The cultural dynamic of machismo is widely acknowledged. In particular, it circulates among AIDS educators as a factor to consider when teaching safer sex. These gender relations among Latinos and Chicanos are typically and simplistically presented as "cultural differences" with little other explanation. By omission, this implies that this behavior is somehow essential or even biologically specific to the culture. (And, importantly, Latinos and Chicanos are often pinpointed for their systems of rigid gender inequality as though such inequality was not also widespread in the dominant white, middle-class culture.)

Recent literature on Latino and Chicano gender relations challenges the "cultural differences" model. Zinn, for example, argues that social-structural factors explain these differences.[37] These include such factors as the economic position of the ethnic group in relation to the dominant culture and whether the man and/or the woman is employed and in what types of jobs. Chafetz suggests that the pattern of male dominance typically described as Latino or Chicano is perhaps more accurately described as working class: "More than most other Americans, the various Spanish speaking groups in this country (Mexican American, Puerto Rican, Cuban) . . . stress dominance, aggressiveness, physical prowess and other stereotypical masculine traits. Indeed the masculine sex role for this group is generally described by reference to the highly stereotyped notion of machismo. In fact, a strong emphasis on masculine aggressiveness and dominance may be characteristic of most groups in the lower ranges of the socioeconomic ladder.[38]

Zinn emphasizes that it is important not to ignore that male dominance exists among Latinos and Chicanos but that this dynamic should not be explained as an essential cultural difference.

How powerful is machismo in contemporary Latino and Chicano relationships? How much do men control sexual relationships, sexual decision making, and even women's sexuality? While there is some disagreement about this, most researchers acknowledge that such factors as acculturation and the women's movement have had an impact. In a recent study of black and Hispanic (85 percent of them Puerto Rican) women, Kline found that both groups demonstrated an enormous amount of independence—including economic independence—and defiance of traditional gender roles.[39] This was particular true for the Hispanic women. One woman described her freedom of reproductive choice: "It would be my ultimate decision. It's my life and not his, and I am carrying the baby. So it would be my choice. So whether he liked it or not, I would have an abortion."[40]

Kline also found that many Hispanic women were able to use cultural stereotypes to their advantage in sexual decision making. One woman reported, "Latin men have this macho problem. And I was able to convince him. I told him about our problem. I told him that I love you and you love me. We have a child. You are out there using drugs. I don't use drugs. When you make love to me you pass the drug on to me. I told him if you love me, you have to use a condom."[41]

These data don't disprove that there is gender inequality and should not be used to ignore male power and dominance. They are studies of small samples and cannot be widely generalized. Nevertheless, they are important because they point to the complexity of power negotiation in heterosexual relationships. They suggest to us that, despite a broader social context of male dominance, women may be able to exert resistance and wield power as well. They also suggest that social structure, rather than simply cultural factors, largely accounts for gender relations among different groups. We cannot predict, based simply on culture, how gender relations are configured within a given group. Indeed, Cromwell found that among blacks, Latinos, and whites, there was a range of relationship structures, from matriarchal and patriarchal to egalitarian.[42]

Probably the most accurate lesson to be drawn from the various data in this chapter is that gender matters to sexuality, but how it matters tends to vary. Gender shapes rather than determines sexuality. And given the social, political, and economic changes of the last few decades, including the growing influence of feminism, the ways in which gender shapes sexuality are not always clear. Nevertheless, individuals make most sexual decisions as part of a couple. And for heterosexuals, gender differences continue to be determinants in such areas as level of sexual activity, types of sexual behavior, meanings attributed to sex, and the practice of contraception and safer sex. Given these factors, gender matters to sexuality educators as well.

Sexual Language, Conversational Strategies, and Communication Patterns

The United Nations Conference on Population and Development that met in Cairo in September 1994 was the focus of much controversy. Delegates from diverse nations and cultures were in disagreement on such thorny issues as abortion and sexuality. Once they reached consensus, however, they faced an enormous unforeseen hurdle: translation of the final plan into their own languages.

English phrases proved to be difficult to translate into many other languages either because there are no equivalent cultural concepts and therefore no suitable terms or because the terms are considered offensive. For example, the phrases "sex education" and "sexual health" were difficult to translate into Arabic since almost any word derived from "sex" is deeply offensive in that language. Similarly, "single-parent household" had no comparable Arabic phrase, since it is taboo in Arabic society for unmarried women to raise children. Both the Chinese and French translators complained that "empowerment for women" was nearly impossible to translate. The French finally settled on the wordy "renforcement du pouvoir d'action des femmes" (reinforcement of the power of women to act), although some complained that it is a technically incorrect use of "renforcement." The French translator finally quipped, "I'm not sufficiently empowered to change it."[1]

These difficulties illustrate how language is another area of our work in which culture has an enormous impact. Communication, in fact, is a domain of primary concern for sexuality educators. Ultimately it is the quality of our communication that determines the effectiveness of our programs. Several points are particularly relevant for sexuality educators. First, the choice of appropriate language is an ongoing challenge when working with any group. Second, the conversational strategies of both educator and audience can shape the outcome of a program. Third, groups have distinct communication patterns concerning sexuality, and these dynamics can affect our work. This chapter will review some central issues regarding cultural diversity and these different levels of communication.

Sexual Language

Language is perhaps the most vital yet taken-for-granted aspect of sexuality education. It is the very foundation of our communication with others. Yet educators who might spend days designing a workshop often give little consideration to the question of appropriate language. We ignore language to our peril, however, since it plays such a central role in shaping and defining all that we consider to be sexuality.

Language is not neutral, either culturally or politically. Nor is it simply a tool that is natural and fairly universal. Rather our words, symbols, images, and metaphors are deeply reflective of our social norms and cultural values. And it is historical; language and its meanings change over time.

In English, sexual language derives from two basic sources: medicine and street slang. There are also some sexual euphemisms, like "it" and "down there." Our choices of appropriate language, therefore, are severely limited. If we want to discuss body parts, the technical and formal terms "penis" and "vagina" will certainly be appropriate in many circumstances, especially in educational settings with European-American, middle-class adults. These terms may fit less well in intimate settings or in informational materials for adolescents. Slang may be more fitting in these situations.

Yet most of our slang reflects the values and biases of street cultures. So while sometimes "vagina" might be an awkward term to use, many people feel uncomfortable with slang alternatives such as "cunt" or "fish bucket." The absence of a wider range of sexual languages reflects deep cultural anxieties about sexuality. It also reinforces sexual silence, since people will tend not to speak without a familiar and comfortable set of terms.

A close examination of both medical and slang sexual languages reveals how they are both politically and historically constructed. Much of our medical vocabulary derives from the work of sexologists during the last one hundred years. Sexologists, in particular, have invented a wide vocabulary related to sexual categories and problems. The terms are political because, although they appear to be neutral and scientific, they reveal assumptions and biases about what is sexual and which sexualities are acceptable and unacceptable. For example, the famous sex researchers William Masters and Virginia Johnson invented a set of categories and terms for what they described as common sexual problems—problems that included premature ejaculation and impotence in men and painful intercourse and failure to achieve orgasm in women.

Critics argue that Masters and Johnson created an entire system and language of sexual problems that is biased due to an emphasis on intercourse as the central focus of sexuality.[2] Every sexual dysfunction they invented concerns a failure at coitus. There is, for example, no category of dysfunction for someone unable to masturbate. Some feminists have claimed that medical sexual language represents a male-dominated view of sexuality in that what is considered sexual is only genitally oriented, with intercourse as the ultimate and most important sexual act. The importance of this issue for sexuality educators is the recognition that language is not neutral but rather reinforces dominant ideas about sexuality.

Medical terminology has also changed over time to reflect cultural and political changes in our sex/gender system. Categories of sexual problems have evolved or disappeared depending on social and medical values. For example, masturbatory insanity was a very popular sexual dysfunction of the nineteenth century, with the "onanist" a deviant figure who practiced excessive self-abuse.[3] These ideas collapsed in the early twentieth century; in fact, by the 1960s and 1970s, sexologists were celebrating the health benefits of masturbation. Significantly, however, they failed to invent terms to describe either the masturbatory enthusiast or one who fails to masturbate. This, as noted, reflects the sex researchers' bias toward intercourse.

Medical language has evolved in ways that both shape and reinforce changing sexual scripts for women. The change has mostly centered on notions of sexual desire and orgasm, two issues that have historically been the source of deep cultural concern and anxiety. In the early part of this century, for example, psychiatrists identified the "hypersexual female" as a psychopath who could not control aggressive sexual desire.[4] This deviant figure vanished later in the century, as desire in women became more acceptable due to a broad range of social, economic, and political changes. In fact, near the end of the twentieth century the most common sexual dysfunction for women is inhibited sexual desire, reflecting the contemporary idea that sexual pleasure is central and lack of desire is a disorder.[5]

The changes and reversals of medical sexual language can be read as metaphors. They do not result from advances in scientific knowledge but rather reflect social and political tensions that emerge in our sex/gender system. As we discussed earlier, ideas about acceptable levels of women's sexual desire have changed continually over the last centuries. And the idea of dangerous and excessive desire in women that was reflected in the diagnosis of hypersexual female is making a comeback in the late twentieth century "sex addict."[6] Medical sexual language is not an objective terminology but one that sends powerful messages about what is acceptable and what (and who) is deviant.

Sexual slang, on the other hand, harbors no pretensions of objectivity. Sexuality educators are typically well versed in slang, since a common educational activity is the brainstorming session. One goal of this exercise, in which group participants shout out slang terms for such words as penis and vagina, is to demonstrate the enormous range of words for the genitalia compared to other body parts—which illustrates the cultural salience of, and anxiety about, these areas of the body.

Another important goal of the sexual slang exercise is to examine the imagery embedded in the terms. Slang tends to reflect the double standard applied to female and male bodies and sexuality. Terms for the penis reflect its image as often powerful (ramrod, shaft) or even threatening (gun, weapon) but clearly valued (family jewels). While the vagina may be described as benignly desirable (honey pot), other terms overwhelmingly reflect absence (hole, slot) or disgust (dead fish, stink hole). The terms for intercourse similarly reflect our cultural equation of sex with intercourse, particularly that which is aggressive and male-controlled. "Banging," "nailing," and "gang bang" depict an act in which men overpower, dominate, or even hurt women. Sexual slang, like medical language, reflects broader social norms and cultural values.

Sexual language is of concern for sexuality educators not just because of implicit values but also because cultures deal with sexual language in very different ways. There are differences, for example, in the acceptability of direct sexual communication or explicit language. This is a complicated issue, and one that cannot be answered with simple statements about which cultures are sexually open and which are sexually conservative. Generalizations are difficult to make, because there is so little sophisticated research on culture and sexuality that takes into account both internal tensions and differences based on such factors as gender and age. Nevertheless, it is important to review some of the central issues concerning culture and sexual openness and explicitness.

The dominant, European-American, middle-class sexual culture has grown increasingly public and open throughout this century. This can be seen in both the growing commercialization and visibility of sex in pornography and prostitution since the late nineteenth century and the increase in medical writing by sex researchers that has resulted in widespread popular coverage of sexual issues in magazines and newspapers. Pornography, advertising, novels, television shows, and movies have all become increasingly sexually explicit since the 1950s. Growing sexual openness is one aspect of what historians John D'Emilio and Estelle Freedman call "the sexualized society" of the late twentieth century.[7]

These broader changes have not affected all groups equally. Even among European Americans, who comprise the dominant racial culture discussed previously, there are differences. Gender may be one source of difference, as researchers have suggested variations in male and female sexual vocabularies.[8] In one study, women preferred a narrower range of sexual terms across all contexts, as compared to males. Women consistently used "penis," "vagina," "make love," or pet names for the penis like "Oscar." Ethnicity may also influence sexual communication among whites. One study found a very open and explicit level of sexual communication in Polish families compared to the intense privacy of the group that, at the time of this study, is called Slovak Americans.[9]

We can see, then, that different groups exhibit different cultural patterns relative to the openness and explicitness of their sexual communication and language. Sexuality and AIDS educators have been particularly interested in patterns among urban communities of color. Norms among these groups have often been superficially described as sexual conservatism among Asian Americans and Latinos and sexual liberalism among African Americans. Although there is a very small literature on culture and sexual communication, it can help us expand these generalizations.

Whatever differences might exist among cultures are, of course, not the result of inherent or essential factors. Different patterns emerge from different material conditions in the histories of social groups. This is certainly true for sexual culture among African Americans. Open and explicit sexual communication is an oft-noted characteristic of black culture. Fullilove and her colleagues note: "In community settings like barbershops, beauty parlors, and bars, sex is a frequent topic of conversation. The common profane language in the black community—'fuck,' 'suck my dick,' etc.—is concerned with sexual activity. More subtle allusions are frequent as well, for example, the delightful pun in the name of the professional basketball player, 'Magic' Johnson (johnson is a synonym for penis in the black community). Talking about sex is important and commonplace."[10]

Other scholars have noted the important roles of dance and such music as the blues and rap in the sexual socialization of black youth. As Joseph and Lewis point out, however, the sexual messages in cultural expression reflect the realities of black life. Blues singers taught black women about sexuality in the black community: "the nature of and ways to deal with two-timing men; men mistreating women; cheating women; women longing for their men and willing to pay any price to be with their men; men who can't quite measure up sexually; the hardships associated with being a poor Black woman; and the glorification of sex."[11] The fluidity of explicit sexual communication is related to social and economic specifics in African-American history, including the legacy of slavery, the impact of the black church, and economic hardship and discrimination.

Cultures are complex, changeable, and stratified by factors like gender and social class, so it would be a mistake to overstate the acceptability of explicit sexual discussion in the African-American community. More research is needed to examine the level of communication within relationships, for example. Fullilove has hinted that, despite a norm of openness in the culture, many people in her study found sexual discussions with their partners to be difficult. It is also possible that black men might attach different sexual meanings to slang or negotiate sexual communication differently than black women. Although there is much room for clarification and elaboration, there does seem to be much agreement on a quality of open and explicit sexual communication among African Americans.

Other cultural groups who comprise a significant segment of the U.S. population—Asian Americans, Latinos, and Chicanos—have been noted for their reticence concerning sexual matters. AIDS educators frequently remark on this dynamic in the context of planning programs and interventions concerning safer sex and condom use. They fear, and rightfully so, that explicit language might offend audience members or make the participants so uncomfortable as to render the message ineffective. This is an important concern, but it should also be noted that cultures are dynamic, and socialization into cultural patterns can vary according to such factors as social class, age, and length of time in this country.

As with African Americans, patterns of sexual communication, in particular sexual reticence, among Asian Americans, Latinos, and Chicanos are grounded in the socio-historical circumstances of each group. Difficulty or unwillingness to discuss sex does not mean the same things, or come from the same sources, in Asian American culture as in Latino. This is particularly true given the enormous diversity within these racial categories. The category of Asian and Pacific Islander, for example, comprises more than forty groups, each with distinct cultures, many of whom have nothing in common and have traditionally been enemies.[12] Latinos also come from many countries, races, and regions and comprise different cultures.[13] Generalizations, then, are fraught with complication.

It is important to note that unwillingness to engage in explicit sexual discussion does not mean the absence of sexual communication. For example, many scholars have noted the difficulty Latino and Chicano men have with directly discussing sexuality or AIDS. Conversations are often deflected with jokes.[14] Yet, as de la Vega notes, Latinos communicate abundantly about sex, albeit in indirect and nonverbal ways.[15] Indirectness is also a characteristic of communication among many Asian and Pacific Island groups. Despite these dynamics, which can be a challenge for sexuality educators, who often depend on explicitness, sexual communication does occur within these many groups.

Given the diverse ways in which culture and politics shape sexual language, the sexuality educator is faced with several tasks. There is no simple formula for finding appropriate sexual terminology. Each educator must assess the audience, message, and context in light of his or her own background and skills and, unfortunately, make choices without benefit of a truly rich and evocative sexual language. We can, however, point out the values and biases in sexual language, both medical and slang (see The Question of Slang), as an important aspect of the educational process. Sexuality educators who share the race or ethnicity of their audience may face an easier task but must still be aware of differences by gender, age, and social class. We can never assume similarities in either the sexual communication patterns or the meanings we attach to sexual language.

The Question of Slang

Sexuality educators who work with youth frequently face the question of whether or not to use slang in their work. Educators are virtually unanimous in the conviction that young people must learn the more formal, medical sexual vocabulary and that, in most cases, this is the appropriate language for the classroom. There are circumstances, however, when slang is more appropriate and effective. The challenge is to determine when and how.

It is useful to view slang as a cultural language. It typically emerges from youth culture, and specific terms, expressions, and, most importantly, meanings can vary by region, gender, and race and ethnicity. Sexuality educator Pam Wilson has noted that the meaning of the same slang term can vary between black and white youth.[1] Slang also evolves rapidly; even small changes in wording or meaning assume tremendous importance and mark the individual who makes an error as terminally unhip.

Because slang is a cultural language, there are both advantages and disadvantages to its use by sexuality educators. Even if educators choose not to use sexual slang, the young people they work with will certainly use it to communicate among themselves and will sometimes bring it into the classroom. Lack of knowledge about the most current sexual slang will put the sexuality educator at a definite disadvantage. When sexuality educators demonstrate that they understand the slang of their audience it can be the ground for connection between groups who are separate by age.

Sexuality educators can probably most safely and effectively use slang in situations where it is unclear who the speaker is. This is specifically the case with educational materials like brochures and posters. The message is embedded in a static medium and can easily be read as coming from another adolescent. In Boston, for example, posters that advocated condom use among young black men with the phrase "Don't forget your jimmy hat" were highly successful. Slang can target, and connect a message with, a particular cultural group. (On the other hand, these posters were controversial among some adults who found them inappropriate. This is another familiar battle for sexuality educators.)

The major hazards for sexuality educators in using slang lie in the dangers of cross-cultural communication. It is particularly risky for members of dominant groups to use the language of nondominant groups, since it can be interpreted as, and frequently is, cultural appropriation. Most sexuality educators, by nature of their age, are in a more powerful position than the youth they teach. The risk of resentment is even greater if the educator attempts to use the slang of a different racial or ethnic group. Even if the slang is used correctly, audience members may feel violated.

Another compelling danger of using slang is the disastrous possibility of using it incorrectly. A most public example of this occurred in the 1992 presidential campaign when George Bush, trying to indicate his enthusiasm for debating Bill Clinton, exclaimed, "Let's get it on." This is, of course, a familiar sexual slang expression, made even more popular by the Marvin Gaye song of the same name, that indicates a wish to begin sexual activity. There were very few critics who pointed this out; most commentators were either too polite or similarly ignorant. Nonetheless, for weeks George Bush appeared in television sound bites challenging Bill Clinton with the phrase, "Let's get it on." Most sexuality educators will wisely avoid risking credibility in this fashion with a young audience.

Slang is not neutral but indicative of values about sexuality and gender. This raises important pedagogical questions for sexuality educators, not simply about whether to use slang ourselves but also concerning ways to address the use of slang by our students. Sexuality educator Deborah Roffman has described her work in the classroom helping students to see how the images and metaphors in sexual baseball terminology reflect a sexual double standard and depict sexual activity as an exploitive game.[2] She helps students analyze the deeper meanings of terms like "walk" (what he does if she gets pregnant), "error" (not using birth control, or birth control failures), and "slug out" (when she keeps him from "scoring" for the entire game).

Roffman uses slang itself as the basis for a sexuality education lesson, one in which students begin to examine their own value systems and those of the dominant culture. This is an important technique, especially given the inadequacy of our sexual languages. It is a method that should be used cautiously, however, since the educator runs the risk of offending and alienating the students. This is especially possible if the educator is examining the slang used by a specific racial or ethnic group. Analysis of the values in the slang may be seen as racist, particularly if the educator is from a different culture.

[1] Pamela M. Wilson, "Black Culture and Sexuality," *Journal of Social Work and Human Sexuality* 4, no. 3 (1986): 29–46.
[2] Deborah M. Roffman, "The Power of Language: Baseball as a Sexual Metaphor in American Culture," *SIECUS Report* 19, no. 5 (1991): 1–6.

Conversational Strategies

As sexuality educators, we rely on group participation. Because of the nature of the material, the most effective programs are often those that are heavily interactive. Small group discussions are a particularly common structure for training sessions. Since research indicates that skill building is an important component of sexuality education, most programs incorporate role-playing exercises and other opportunities for rehearsal and interaction.

The most effective sexuality educators are skilled in group facilitation, ever alert to the dynamics in the room. But even the most experienced of us have led groups or classes that felt out of control. Speakers wander off the topic. Others try to dominate the discussion. Sometimes it is impossible to encourage silent participants to speak. Facilitating a group can be challenging and exhausting. Cultural analysis can be a useful tool for thinking about group interaction.

Group dynamics can be influenced by cultural differences. An individual's conversational characteristics—for example, level of directness or indirectness, volume of speech, tendency to interrupt, argue, or remain silent—are not necessarily idiosyncratic mannerisms. Instead, a growing body of research indicates that these styles are shaped by culture. While individuals certainly have distinct personalities, their patterns and preferred modes of interacting in groups are also affected by their social worlds. Race and ethnicity, gender, and social class can all shape conversational strategies.

Like sexual language, conversational strategies are not neutral. Some styles are valued more than others. Specifically, conversational styles of groups with more social power are considered the normal and standard mode of interaction. Differences are considered deviations, and groups can be stigmatized on this basis. One aspect of anti-Semitism, for example, is the attribution to Jewish people of the characteristics of loudness and pushiness.[16] The "inscrutable Oriental" is another negative stereotype based on difference in conversational strategy.

Speakers from dominant groups can also use conversational strategies to reinforce their power within a group. It is these dynamics to which sexuality educators will want to be most attentive. Such maneuvers are not necessarily conscious or intentionally manipulative, although on occasion they certainly are. Often, however, it is simply that by being more adept at particular conversational strategies, members of dominant groups are able to take up more space and wield more power in groups.

Gender differences have been the subject of considerable research in this area. Sociolinguist Deborah Tannen argued in her best-selling book *You Just Don't Understand* that men and women frequently have misunderstandings because of differences in conversational styles.[17] Tannen's work is important for us not only because she emphasizes communication differences but also because her work has been so popularized. Because she has brought these ideas into the mainstream, students are often familiar with them and quite eager to discuss their implications. It is important to note, however, that her research has been the subject of some criticism. After a brief review of some of this work in the area of culture and communication, I will examine these issues.

Many researchers have identified gender differences in conversation. Men tend to approach a conversation as a contest for status rather than as an approach to connection; they interrupt more and assume the role of the lecturer, with the woman as the listener. Studies have repeatedly found that in public settings like meetings and classrooms, men speak more often and for longer periods of time. As Tannen notes, "Many men are more comfortable than most women in using talk to claim attention."[18] These findings have important implications for group facilitators, for we will want to be aware of ways in which men might take up more space or use conversation as a way of dominating others in the group.

Ethnic groups may vary widely in their styles of involvement in conversations, including pacing of speech, pausing after speakers, and overlapping speech. Tannen characterizes two conversational styles.[19] High-involvement conversants are those who leave little or no time after someone speaks before beginning to talk and who may interrupt or overlap with the speaker. On the other hand, high-considerateness conversants favor longer pauses after speakers, do not overlap or interrupt, and favor a slower pace.

Tannen notes the possibility for misunderstanding between speakers who are from these different groups. While high-involvement speakers may intend to show enthusiasm and connection by jumping in and overlapping, high-considerateness speakers can feel disrupted, cut off, and irritated. On the other hand, high-involvement speakers may interpret the long pauses and slow pace of high-considerateness speakers as boredom rather than politeness.

The categories of high involvement and high considerateness are defined in relation to each other, not in the abstract. Tannen has noted that while New Yorkers tend toward high involvement compared to the slower pace of Californians, most Americans generally become overlappers and interrupters in relation to Scandinavians, who in turn differ among themselves. Swedes and Norwegians can seem high involvement in relation to the reticent Finns.

There has been some disagreement over how best to describe communication differences. These conflicts center around the problems of power and dominance. For example, some critics read Tannen's work as simply a description of conversational styles, as though communication were comparable to choice of hairstyle or wardrobe. They complain that Tannen ignores the very real power differences between women and men that are reinforced by male conversational dominance. Instead, they argue, she interprets dominance as misunderstanding.[20] Tannen has addressed her critics by explaining that her emphasis on cultural styles does not preclude an analysis about the ways in which certain cultures can exercise dominance. Interested readers may want to explore this debate for themselves. Meanwhile, we will want to stay very attuned in our classrooms to the ways in which cultural differences in communication can result in some individuals being more powerful and dominant in the group.

Cultural generalizations about conversational strategies should be interpreted with caution. We need more research on how race and ethnicity, gender, age, region, and class affect styles. And it is crucial to understand the impact of multiple and intersecting cultural identifications. For example, how are strategies employed in an interaction between an Chinese man and a woman from New York? He is from a high-considerateness ethnic group but a dominant gender category, and she is in a subordinate gender position but from a high-involvement region. And there are clearly other identities that might be factored in, such as class and age. We are at an early but important stage of understanding these conversational strategies.

Sexuality educators will want to develop an awareness of our own conversational strategies, not just the cultural style differences of audience members. As the teacher or facilitator, the educator has a great deal of power to impose her conversational style and to set patterns of communication. It is useful to recognize our own strategies of pacing, silence or dominance, and interrupting or overlapping and to discern how they can best fit with the dynamics of any specific group.

Underpinning issues of cultural differences in sexual language and conversational strategies are questions of meanings. Who speaks, who is spoken to, what gets spoken, and how does it get interpreted? As should be abundantly clear by now, disruptions and breakdowns can occur at any stage of the communication process. One speaker may talk about "sex," and the listener imagines very different activities than those intended by the speaker. People in conversation can have quite different notions of the meaning of an interaction or, indeed, of whether it happened at all.

Sociologist Janet Kahn showed that within families, parents recall many more discussions about sexuality than their children remember.[21] Sons, in particular, don't recall most of the conversations their mothers swear took place. Also, sons tend not to perceive the imposition of parental rules about sexuality, while daughters remember them quite clearly. If these gaps in communication and interpretation occur frequently within families, we can be certain that they take place during our educational programs as well.

There is no simple formula for addressing the challenge of cultural difference in language and communication. Both awareness of these patterns and cross-cultural literacy will enable each educator to fashion more effective approaches for each specific audience.

Culture and Risk:
A Contextual View

Why do some people continually engage in unhealthy behavior? Why, given the risk of such dangerous or unpleasant consequences as infection or unwanted pregnancy, do individuals have intercourse without condoms or contraception? How can people be persuaded to change their behavior? Is it sufficient to give them information? Does fear work? Questions such as these, which highlight the problems of risk and behavior change, underpin sexuality education.

Sexuality education has its roots in the social hygiene movements of the late nineteenth and early twentieth century. These initiatives were organized around specific problems that included the eradication of what were then called venereal diseases. Early hygiene education was largely didactic, and practitioners focused on giving information about diseases and how to prevent them.[1] The health education and sexuality education models that evolved from these movements maintained a strong emphasis on personal behavior, lifestyle, and health-related habits. Today, the behavior change model of health education is one of the most common. It is an approach that, through providing information and offering preventive services, aims to effect change in the lives of individuals so that they will be healthier.

Behavior change is a central goal of most sexuality education programs. We want people to practice safer sex. Or, in the case of teenagers, some educators would like them not to practice sex at all. We have programs to teach decision-making skills and negotiation skills. We have students rehearse different sexual scripts. Ultimately the goal is safety; no one should be coerced into sex, contract a disease from sexual activity, or wind up with an unwanted pregnancy. It is important to recognize that this emphasis on safety is by no means the only goal of good educational programs today. Comprehensive sexuality education addresses the broadest realm of sexuality, including intimacy, relationships, body image, personal values, and self-esteem. However, controversies over teaching about sexuality has had the unfortunate result of narrowing many programs. Educators who want to teach comprehensive curricula often find themselves involved in bitter battles, or nervous schools boards limit their programs. Political pressures, then, have conspired to keep many programs locked into virtually the same emphasis of one hundred years ago: prevention of sexual dangers.

Given this historical focus on prevention and safety, sexuality educators have searched for models to predict how and why people change their behavior. Generally, they have looked in the direction of psychology and public health education. These disciplines have yielded important insights about how individual attitudes and belief systems affect health-related behaviors. These models have significantly influenced the vision and design of most comprehensive sexuality education programs. In their focus on individual health, they reinforce the behaviorism of sexuality education, the interest in health choices and behavior changes, and the attention to "risky" behaviors and people "at risk."

The Health Belief Model

Perhaps the best-known formulation about such behavioral choices is the Health Belief Model (HBM). The HBM, first developed in the 1950s in response to problems with health screening and prevention measures, was more fully elaborated in the 1970s by sociologist

Marshall Becker.[2] It is a psychosocial model that attempts to explain and predict why individuals do or do not engage in specific health-related activities. The Health Belief Model has been applied to such problems as immunization, screening, self-examination, dental practice, and diabetic care. For example, researchers have assessed how well the HBM predicts an individual's likelihood of obtaining a flu vaccination. In the last decade the Health Belief Model has been adopted by AIDS researchers and educators for its possible utility in predicting the practice of safer sex and drug use behaviors.

The Health Belief Model is a behavioral theory suggesting that action depends on two factors: how much an individual values a specific goal, and the person's perception of whether a particular action will achieve that goal. There are four components of the HBM, which, when combined, predict whether or not a person will engage in a health-related activity. First, an individual must *perceive susceptibility* to a particular condition. She must, for example, think that it is possible that she could get HIV. Second, the individual must *perceive severity* of the condition. That is, she must believe HIV has serious consequences. Third, the person must *perceive benefits* in the preventive actions available to her. She must think that condom use will be both possible and effective against contracting HIV. Finally, the *perceived barriers* are crucial. If she finds that condom use is unpleasant, embarrassing, expensive, or otherwise difficult, it will undermine the likelihood of her engaging in this particular preventive behavior. In some respects, then, the Health Belief Model is based on a theory of rational choice in which individuals engage in cost-benefit analyses.

The Health Belief Model has been popular because it theorizes that behavior is not random or irrational. Rather, it offers a predictive model based on an assumption that people act purposefully and in their own best interests. Importantly, the Health Belief Model offers tangible direction to health and sexuality educators who seemingly need only to target the four basic elements. Educators must convince their audience members that they are susceptible to a particular condition, that it is serious, and that they can take effective action with few obstacles. Although in practice this task can prove quite formidable and unwieldy (think, for example, of teenagers and contraception use), the HBM does offer a road map.

Despite its utility, however, the Health Belief Model has significant limitations. The most important, for our purposes, is that it neglects the social and cultural context, examining the individual almost in a vacuum. This emphasis is not surprising since it is, as its developers quite readily attest, a model that foregrounds individual beliefs and attitudes. And researchers did add to the HBM what they call "modifying factors," such as "age, sex, race, ethnicity, etc."[3] The peripheral addition of these factors, unfortunately, has not proven sufficient to offset the individualizing bias of the Health Belief Model. In fact, several studies have found that the attitudinal factors in the Health Belief Model did not successfully explain risk behavior for HIV, with one study finding that the factors accounted for significantly less than half of the health-related variability among gay and bisexual men.[4] The shortcomings of the HBM and, by extension, of the concepts of risk and behavior change are crucial to sexuality educators who wish to develop comprehensive and culturally sensitive programs.

The most central question for educators is, What explains peoples' behavior? Educational interventions contain inherent and often unexamined assumptions about why individuals act and how they change. Condom availability programs, for example, rest on the assumption that *access* is a crucial factor in safer sex practice among students. Reliance on brochures and billboards signals a belief that imparting *information* (components one and two of the Health Belief Model) about a problem like HIV or unwanted pregnancy will motivate behavior change. Showing slides of people dying from AIDS-related diseases assumes that people will change their behavior out of *fear*. Like these, most ideas about motivation and behavior focus narrowly on aspects of the individual person. Yet this is only a piece of the behavior change puzzle.

Social constructionists offer a more complicated perspective on sexual behavior and risk taking. They suggest that sexuality is not just the expression of an internal drive but, rather, the product of a person's social and cultural worlds. Sexual choices and decisions are informed by the complex meanings the individual attaches to such factors as sexuality, relationships, families, and the physical body. Meanings are historical (they change over time) and sociocultural (they vary according to an individual's social location and cultural norms). For sexuality educators who adopt this perspective, the bad news is that this is a more complicated view of sexuality that belies simple solutions to the problem of behavior change. The good news is that the very complexity of this approach gives us a more sophisticated understanding of how individuals operate within their social groups and therefore offers the possibility of developing truly effective educational interventions. The advantages of this approach are apparent in two examples that are of great importance to sexuality educators: contraception use among adolescent girls and safer sex practices among women.

Teenage Girls, Contraception, and Risk

A significant number of teenagers have sexual intercourse without using birth control. Research in the mid-1980s revealed that 82 percent of teen pregnancies were unintended; the younger the girl the more likely it was unplanned.[5] One study showed that among adolescent girls who did not want to become pregnant, only 31 percent reported using condoms.[6] Why? Do they lack information about contraceptives, or are they unable to obtain them? Over the decades, researchers have suggested a number of explanations. Underpinning each of them are assumptions about sexuality, gender, and the origins of "risk taking."

There have been important feminist contributions in the last twenty years to the discussion of teenage girls and noncontraception. This research has significantly reconceptualized the traditional literature by viewing girls as sexual subjects who, although constrained by certain cultural and material limitations, act on the basis of a variety of complicated factors. These perspectives challenge prior notions that an adolescent's unwanted pregnancy is the result of either ignorance about contraception or of unresolved psychological conflicts.

Kristin Luker, in her book *Taking Chances: Abortion and the Decision Not to Contracept*, argued that not using birth control is, as her title reflects, a purposeful decision. According to Luker, young unmarried women make a decision not to contracept because their goals are more complicated than the simple prevention of pregnancy. Contraception and pregnancy hold multiple meanings for these women, and they assess their options and choices in a rational fashion. This is, in certain respects, similar to the cost-benefit analysis suggested in the second half of the Health Belief Model.

Luker suggests that contraception use may be "costly" and that young women secure certain benefits or gains from a pregnancy even if they do not want to bear a child right then. For example, many women could not tolerate the explicit acknowledgment of their sexual activity that is inherent in planning and using contraception. They want to avoid being seen, as one girl put it, as a "sexual service station."[7] On the other hand, a pregnancy may heighten a girl's sense of self-worth, reinforce her female identity, and offer her proof of her fertility. Other women told Luker that the pregnancy forced the male partner to define his level of commitment. One young woman said, "You always wonder how well a fiancé or a boy friend will react to what society says is a responsibility of his. Will he freak out, say 'get away,' or will he be loving? He became more loving, and so I think for us a pregnancy makes you work out a lot of things with each other."[8] Clearly, then, the use of contraception emerges as much more than a simple preventive act and is instead revealed as an activity with a range of complicated meanings to girls.

An important component of Luker's theoretical analysis is her adoption of the risk-taking model. This allows her to position women as agents who decide on a course that they then negotiate through risky terrain, rather than passively awaiting their fate. This framework of risk-taking and its connotation of power was new to this discussion when Luker introduced it in 1975. By the 1990s, however, our field is dominated by notions of "risk," "risky sex," and "risk groups." From this vantage point, it is clearer that the conceptual framework of risk-taking is fraught with complications.

Risk is a term that has assumed multiple meanings. It derives its technical meaning from epidemiology, in which risk is merely the possibility of a consequence. For example, researchers examine smoking and the risk of lung cancer or heart disease. Because most of these possible consequences are negative, however, risk has taken on a popular connotation of danger or badness. "Risky sex," for example, is considered inherently inappropriate and dangerous whether or not there are negative consequences such as HIV infection. It has taken only one small step to get to "risk groups," in which danger and disease are viewed as embedded in the group or culture rather than in specific behaviors. In the AIDS epidemic, gay men and Haitians have been treated as though the possibility of contracting HIV came from their membership in these cultural groups rather than from specific sexual or drug using practices. Whether applied to behaviors or individuals, then, *risk* is a term that is overburdened with negative value judgments.

Another shortcoming of the risk-taking framework is its tendency to individualize behavior. As with Luker's use of it, the model of risk taking can emphasize the power of a decision maker rather than the passivity of one driven by internal conflicts. But, typically, the risk-taking lens offers only the view of an individual person assessing her personal and specific risks and benefits. Again, as in the Health Belief Model, the risk taker is viewed as operating in a vacuum, outside of a broader set of social relations. As we will see more fully later, risk is not an objective assessment made by an individual. And one's "choices" may not actually be choices, because of one's limited options. Perception about risk is, indeed, a set of ideas that one constructs out of one's social circumstances, cultural logics, and material conditions.

Luker's important and groundbreaking work on adolescents who don't contracept was limited because of how the risk-taking framework individualized the women's experiences. Political scientist Rosalind Petchesky broadened this literature with her development of a cultural analysis of noncontraceptive behavior.[9] Petchesky addressed the meaning of pregnancy, contraception, and risk but inserted the crucial question about how social and cultural factors shape a woman's construction of these meanings. According to Petchesky, unwanted pregnancy is not just a result of lack of information or even of access (although certainly these material conditions are important). Nor is noncontraception an individual and rational choice. To understand "unwanted" pregnancy, one must consider broader sets of meanings, values, and relationships in contemporary heterosexual culture.

Petchesky relies on social construction theory to suggest that sexuality, contraception, and pregnancy have no universal meanings. Instead they are given a range of meanings depending on the historical era and a woman's social and cultural circumstances. A young woman's behavior in any of these areas must be considered in the context of several factors. In the dominant culture, these include a double message in which women are commercially sexualized but also idealized as innocent and pure. Further, sexuality is infused with complex meanings in the context of family relationships and connections to young men. In addition, the ways in which an adolescent negotiates these paths and constructs sexual meanings varies by such factors as race, ethnicity, and class.

Because sexuality is not a biological drive but a rich and complicated social arena, young people will not readily respond to simple prevention messages. Sharon Thompson suggests, for example, that sexuality is a domain through which adolescent girls negotiate their emerging identities and begin to separate from their families.[10] In these circumstances, a child may be unwanted, but the actual pregnancy provides the occasion for mapping independence, perhaps for realizing the fantasy of moving out and starting a different life. Or, in rural black families, the pregnancy may be a means for the girl to assert her adult status.

Sexuality is an arena in which both boys and girls rehearse gendered behavior. They try out what it means to be a sexual male or female person in their culture, a process that allows them to feel like an adult. As Petchesky suggests, sexuality may well be the one arena in which teenage women feel the most powerful. Pregnancy also puts a girl in a position of asserting her wishes and needs and negotiating some sort of outcome with her male partner. Contraception, then, would make sexual intercourse safe with regard to pregnancy but would undermine "its efficacy as a medium of self-assertion."[11]

Clearly, if these varied dynamics and meanings motivate sexuality and noncontraception, a young woman will not change her "risky" behavior even with unlimited information and access to birth control. Nor will she define her failure to contracept as risky. Thus, as Luker suggested two decades ago, young women manage their sexual and contraceptive decisions with agency and purpose, even if those choices don't correspond to the wishes of their parents or other authorities. Yet, as Petchesky points out, their "choices" are not free and independently made but rather are constructed out of social and cultural circumstances. What constitutes risky behavior is not universally agreed upon. A risky act for one person may be a gesture of intimacy for someone else.

Women, HIV, and Condom Use

Many of the issues that arise in connection with contraception are similar to the dilemmas posed in relation to women and condom use in the AIDS epidemic. First, it is important to note the problems inherent in targeting women as gatekeepers in sexual activity and ignoring the responsibility of male partners in prevention. This is particularly true for condom use, where it is in relation to the male body that women are being asked to take charge. Second, safer sex, like contraception use, is not a simple behavioral event. It carries diverse meanings bound up with the complexities of sexuality, gender relations, and other social and cultural factors. Condom use cannot be considered except in relation to the entirety of a woman's life.

AIDS researchers and educators have grappled with the question of why women won't insist that their partners use condoms during heterosexual intercourse. It is a seemingly simple, rational, and self-protective act. But like failure to use contraception, large numbers of women have condomless intercourse, seeming to ignore safer-sex messages. In one small study, for example, three-quarters of the women interviewed said they never used condoms. While one woman insisted she always did, she also noted that she had not used a condom the last time she had intercourse.[12] In a larger study of 256 couples in each of which one partner was HIV negative and one was HIV positive, only 48.4 percent used condoms consistently for vaginal and anal intercourse.[13]

This behavior has been puzzling to public health professionals who hold to the Health Belief Model or a variant of it. From their perspective, women should be able to effectively practice safer sex if they have the proper attitudes concerning the severity of, and their susceptibility to, HIV infection. And, indeed, most educational intervention stresses information about HIV/AIDS and helps convince women that they can implement effective prevention measures with few difficulties. Largely, however, these educational efforts have failed.

Current research suggests the limitations of the Health Belief Model as it applies to AIDS and safer sex as well as noncontraception. Information does not change behavior. Often, information does not even change attitudes, according to one study which found that adolescents who knew the details of HIV transmission patterns still refused to share the drinking glass of someone with the infection.[14] Most importantly, attitudes about AIDS and ideas about risk are not entities that exist independently but are, rather, constructed within the broadest and deepest context of one's life.

Those women most likely to contract HIV infection are poor, urban African Americans and Latinas. AIDS education programs must address the specifics of their lives rather than rely on the familiar message developed by white, middle-class professionals that women should pressure their male partners into condom use.[15] Unfortunately, the familiar refrain of this book is that there is little sophisticated cultural research on sexuality. But we can begin to examine some current data on urban women in relation to the Health Belief Model to glimpse how behavior change education might be broadened for greater effectiveness.

The Health Belief Model can be conceptually divided in half. We can loosely designate the first two components, perceived susceptibility and perceived severity, as risk or perceived risk. We can view the second two elements, perceived benefits versus perceived barriers, as the cost-benefit analysis related to an action—in this specific case, condom use. An examination of these two factors reveals that culture is at the center.

Risk

As we saw in the case of young women who don't use birth control, "risk" is not a universally shared concept. Risk is a set of ideas and beliefs about what makes us safe and what puts us in danger. Risk exists within the full context of life. When we note that the meaning of risk varies for different people, it is not to say that certain dangers like HIV are less risky for some than others. It is, rather, to recognize that some individuals and groups attribute different meanings to the immediacy or severity of the threat. Or they evaluate the threat in a way that somehow neutralizes it or makes some aspect of it even desirable. We construct different hierarchies and respond to different dangers. We do not, of course, do this arbitrarily; we do it based on the particulars of our social, cultural, and individual situations.

What Does Risk Mean? The Case of Gay Baths

The responses of different groups and communities to the HIV/AIDS epidemic graphically illustrates how "risk"—its meanings, symbols, and dimensions—is socially constructed. What is risky and danger-ous to one group may be neutral or even beneficial to another. Gay bathhouses have been a site for such contests over meaning.

The escalating popularity of gay baths throughout the 1970s and 1980s was a product of the modern lesbian and gay liberation move-ment. The baths became a social institution in the gay male com-munity, a location for meeting, socializing, and sexual interaction. By the mid 1980s, however, critics charged that the baths were a health hazard in that they facilitated the spread of HIV/AIDS. Controversy raged in many cities over the purposes and functions of the bath-houses. Were they a risk in themselves or were they a site for edu-cation to reduce risk?

Opponents of the baths included many public health officials and some within the gay community itself. They criticized what they saw as promiscuous sexuality and viewed the baths as a vehicle for the spread of AIDS. They supported restrictions or outright closure of bathhouses. Some argued that closing the baths would be an impor-tant symbolic, if not real, gesture in the fight to eliminate AIDS. In sev-eral cities, including New York and San Francisco, they succeeded in closing the baths.

While opponents saw the baths only as sleazy and unsafe sex joints, supporters of the bathhouses, who came mostly from within the gay community, painted a different picture. They saw the bath-houses as enhancing safety for a persecuted minority. Baths, they argued, offered a relatively inexpensive, private, and safe alternative to public cruising and sex in public restrooms. And, signficantly, they were sites for effective safer-sex education. At a minimum, posters and other information were displayed, and condoms were distributed. In some bathhouses, AIDS educators conducted safer-sex information sessions. Closing the baths would only disperse the men to other locations and reduce or eliminate the possibility of education.

Many supporters of the bathhouses understandably saw their closure as an affront to the gay male community. Gay men were in the forefront of developing effective safer-sex education that was sensitive to the sexual values, beliefs, and practices of their community. The restrictions on bathhouses came largely from health officials outside of that community who were either unaware of, or indifferent to, gay male social and sexual systems. The restrictions and closures represented the imposition of one group's definition of risk onto another group.[1]

[1] For additional information on the gay bathhouse controversies, see Stephen Murray and Kenneth Payne, "Medical Policy Without Evidence: The Promiscuity Paradigm and AIDS," *California Sociologist* 11 (1988): 13–54; Ronald Bayer, *Private Acts, Social Consequences* (New York: Free Press, 1989); Ralph Bolton, John Vincke, and Rudolf Mak, "Gay Baths Revisited: An Empirical Analysis," *GLQ: A Journal of Lesbian and Gay Studies* 1, no. 3 (1994): 255–273.

Many observers have noted that African Americans did not prioritize HIV/AIDS as a risk because it was merely one more problem or hardship.[16] And, in fact, it was one that was seemingly less immediate in its impact than hunger, homelessness, or violence. Other factors shape the perception of AIDS risk in the African-American community. Racism certainly contributed to the denial of AIDS among blacks, for the "green monkey" theory of HIV origin implicated African Americans as being deviants who spread the virus (see Chapter Three). As a community, African Americans have denied the risk of AIDS in order to maintain "group pride."[17] As individuals, some blacks have ignored AIDS as a protective strategy, one that allows them to feel less marginal and threatened.[18]

The multiple meanings associated with AIDS—deviance, death, immorality, carelessness—infuse the meanings of risk. It is easy to see, then, how simple risk-prevention messages are inadequate in the face of such powerful constructions. Individuals and communities will not hear and integrate messages about the dangers of HIV when to do so leaves them feeling disempowered and stigmatized. Members of different cultural groups will internalize the notion of risk in ways that are shaped by their social, economic, and political circumstances.

Condoms: To Use or Not to Use

To some extent, condom use is related to one's perception of HIV risk. An individual who does not experience risk is unlikely to use a condom. On the other hand, perception of risk does not guarantee condom use. Just as risk has many meanings, so too does using a condom. If we see condom use only as a simple prevention act, we miss the complicated emotional, relational, economic, and political meanings that influence the likelihood of a condom being used.

The two components of the Health Belief Model that relate directly to such behaviors as condom use involve a cost-benefit analysis. The individual must perceive that condoms will be effective in reducing risk and that using them will not be too difficult. Consistent with this, many HIV prevention programs focus on providing information about the protective benefits of condoms. Others concentrate on access, distributing free condoms at popular neighborhood sites. Some programs acknowledge that one of the "obstacles" to condom use may well be the male partner, and so they attempt to train women in skills to negotiate with or persuade him. All of these efforts are important, yet they still fail to address the broad range of complicated meanings attached to condom use by many women.

Studies of urban Latinas and African-American women confirm that failure to use condoms is not a result of lack of knowledge about prevention or lack of experience with the consequences of HIV. Instead, condoms have assumed particular meanings related to cultural status or relationships that make their use unlikely. These meanings constitute far greater obstacles to safer sex practice than either lack of information or access.

For African-American women, social and cultural factors shape the meaning of condoms just as they do risk perception. Resistance to condom use makes sense in the context in which blacks feel both blamed and stigmatized for HIV. Further, many blacks are rightfully suspicious of the pronouncements of white public health officials, given the legacy of the Tuskegee Syphilis Study (see Chapter Three) and such practices as forced sterilization of women of color. Rejection of condoms can be an assertion of community pride, and "unsafe sex is cast as an act of resistance to white oppression."[19]

Gender relations and the dynamics of relationships also give meaning to condom use. On the most immediate level, condom use is an activity that occurs (or doesn't occur) between a woman and man. Factors related to heterosexuality in general, such as unequal power, and to each particular relationship, for example whether or not the partners are economically independent, will shape the meanings and practice of condom use.

Unequal power affects condom use in several ways. Unlike being on the birth control pill, women cannot assume responsibility for condom use. Men can, and do, refuse to wear them for a range of reasons. Sobo suggests that condom refusal is a way in which African-American men dominate women and boost their own self-esteem.[20] In another study, Latina women said that men refused to use condoms because of values associated with maleness and procreation. One woman said, "Especially Spanish men. Because they feel they're not men."[21] Women have reported physical abuse for insisting on condoms.[22] Condom use becomes the site of a power struggle between women and men over issues concerning sexuality, gender relations, and reproduction.

Other subtle and explicit meanings attach to condom use within a relationship. Condomless sex can connote trust in the partner and fidelity within the relationship. Suggesting condom use may then insult the partner or imply that the woman was unfaithful. Not using a condom can mean commitment to the relationship. The feelings of intimacy and romance attached to condomless sex can be a powerful inducement to practice unsafe sex. And there is some disagreement about the extent to which African-American women derive significant economic support from male partners. Nevertheless, a woman who is financially dependent will be unlikely to insist on condom use if doing so jeopardizes the relationship.[23]

In addition to cultural and relational factors, a woman's individual needs may affect the meanings she attributes to condoms. Sobo suggests that women derive a sense of empowerment from their belief that they can identify "clean" men with whom they don't need to practice safer sex.[24] Their self-esteem is enhanced through what Sobo calls the "wisdom narrative": the ability to tell a "good" man from a "bad" one. Using a condom is like admitting the inability to discern this, so unsafe sex is "an adaptive and defensive practice."[25] It allows the woman to hold on to a powerful inner defense.

Clearly, in light of the diverse and complicated meanings of risk and condom use, behavior change is not easy. Nor is it simple to develop educational interventions that account for these meanings. Nevertheless, there are some approaches that would enhance behavior change programs. The Health Belief Model, which is so central to sexuality and AIDS education, must be broadened from its primary focus on the individual. An individual's attitudes are important, but they are not separate from other aspects of one's life. Attitudes are constructed from one's social, cultural, economic, and political context.

Modes of intervention can be developed that address the deep meanings women hold about sexuality, gender, risk, and prevention. For example, Sobo suggests that rather than forcing a woman to give up the "wisdom narrative" or insisting that she persuade her partner to use condoms, the community needs to reframe the meaning of condom use so that it becomes symbolic of loving and intimate relationships. This would involve adjusting the cultural scripts of urban Latino and African-American heterosexuals in much the same way that gay men began to transform their cultural scenarios about sexuality. Ultimately, as with adolescent pregnancy, social and political changes will be necessary to effect the deepest change. In the meantime, programs that locate behavior change in the complicated social, cultural, and economic realities of people's lives will be the most effective ones.

The examples of adolescent noncontraception and women's safer sex practices clearly illustrate that risk is a social and cultural phenomenon. This is true in two ways. First, different societies and communities single out particular risks for attention while ignoring others. This process is not random; instead, "risks are exaggerated or minimized according to the social, cultural, and moral acceptability of the underlying activities."[26] Second, an individual's social location may increase the risk of certain dangers. For example, communities of color are often the site of toxic waste dumping.[27] And we have seen how gender inequality puts women in a vulnerable position concerning condom use and safer sex. As Jonathan Mann, former director of the World Health Organization's AIDS program said, those who are most at risk for AIDS are those who "belong—before AIDS ever appeared—to a group which is discriminated against, marginalized, stigmatized by, and excluded from society."[28] Our models for behavior change, then, must move beyond the individual not only to account for social and cultural factors but also, as Mann emphasizes, to address the ways in which profound social inequality shapes risk.

. . . .

Family Ties

Families are an important social context in which individuals learn about risk. But families are wildly different; the configurations change through different historical eras and across cultural groups. When we acknowledge that sexuality and the ways in which individuals experience risk are shaped by the family, we can only understand what that really means through a deeper examination of the structures and meanings attached to the family.

In the United States, the nature of the family is changing. The nuclear model of two opposite-sex parents with two or three children, and only two generations under one roof, is largely a historical artifact, an invention of the 1950s.[1] This traditional family, unique to the post–World War II era, was a white, middle-class model. Poor families, the working class, and racial minorities were largely excluded from this American dream.

The most recent Census Bureau figures show that fewer than half of all American families have children, and among those that do, nearly one in three has only one parent. Single motherhood, especially among white women, has increased dramatically since the 1950s. Almost 25 percent of white families are single-parent families, while 63 percent of black families with children have only one parent.[2] Among many, the definition of family has expanded to include lesbian and gay relationships and extended friendship systems. A Census Bureau researcher said, "When we are asked what is the typical family, we usually waffle and say we don't define it."[3] The diverse structure of families is, therefore, an important consideration for sexuality educators.

In the dominant culture, the family now exerts considerably less influence over sexuality than in other historical periods. In colonial times, for example, one's sexuality was vigorously policed by the family and the community.[4] Major social changes like urbanization and industrialization weakened the family's hold over individuals and their sexuality. By the end of the nineteenth century, individuals, especially men, were moving in increasing numbers out of the household and into cities. This afforded more privacy and independence from the observing and controlling gaze of the family. For the first time, individuals were away from their families and able to exercise some autonomy with respect to sexuality and relationships.[5]

The weakening of family control over sexuality intensified throughout the twentieth century among the white middle class. It is important, however, to recognize that this is a European-American, middle-class model and that individuals from other racial and ethnic groups may experience both more family connections and more control over their sexuality by their family. Sexuality educators from the dominant culture, for whom sexuality is highly individual and private, may not even think about assessing the level of control exerted by the family system over sexual behavior and attitudes. Conversely, educators from cultures with strong family traditions may forget that these ties do not hold for many in the U.S. today.

The traditionally close family retains central importance among many groups, particularly immigrants. For example, psychologist Michelle Klopner points out that Haitians have relied on the family in the absence of any other support.[6] Family interdependence is manifested in material and emotional connections among a wide group. The Latino conception of family, for example, includes an extended system of relatives going back several generations. The tight and insular nature of Latino families may offer affection and individual support, especially concerning activities such as child-rearing. Some Latinos, and especially Latinas, may experience constraints from family policing of their sexuality.

Among Asian and Pacific Islanders, the family occupies a prominence that extends well beyond the need for support and safety. Asians stress the needs of the collective or family over those of the individual.[7] Some hypothesize that this allows families greater control over the sexual behavior of their children. Family pressures may also engender enormous anxiety among Asian-American adolescents who begin sexual experimentation.[8] Lesbian and gay youth, who fear disgracing the family, may engage in more anonymous sexual behavior or in activities with those outside of their culture because of family stigmatization.[9]

With government and public interest focused on such issues as welfare reform, teenage pregnancy, urban violence, and drug abuse, the black family has often been targeted as the cause of such problems. Undeniably, African Americans have faced considerable obstacles in forming and maintaining stable families. Under slavery, families were virtually impossible to form and maintain. Ongoing discrimination in employment and housing leaves many blacks in poor, ghetto areas. The infant mortality rate for blacks is double that of whites, and the homicide rate has soared in black neighborhoods. All of these factors contribute to fragmentation of the black family.

Yet for many blacks, the family holds important strengths related to historical traditions. These include "role flexibility (including the fact that black men, in spite of 'macho' images and language, are more likely to share housework than are their white counterparts); extended-kin networks, including effective fostering traditions; parallel institutions, such as black newspapers, churches, and professional organizations; bicultural experiences, languages, and values; racial solidarities; and a tradition of pooling economic resources."[10] These characteristics have important implications for sexuality. Black adolescents come of age sexually not just in a context of racial oppression and family fragmentation; many may have the experience of a strong, extended family in which all adults share responsibility for children.

Families are complicated and diverse systems. They are shaped by cultural factors, such as racial and ethnic tradition, economic factors, such as social-class status, and political factors, such as acceptance or rejection of lesbians and gay men. Families shape the sexuality of the individuals who live in them in complicated ways. Some families are nurturing and supportive of sexual development. Others are silent and fearful, or perhaps overtly abusive. Many families exhibit contradictory patterns; for example, they may outwardly accept sexuality but implicitly, through silence or mixed messages, encourage sexual shame.

The family is the invisible but powerful presence in the classroom. Every lesson gets filtered through earlier messages from the family. The nature of these messages, and the impact they have, will often vary depending on family structure and tradition.

[1] Stephanie Coontz, *The Way We Never Were: American Families and the Nostalgia Trap* (New York: Basic Books, 1992).

[2] "What Is the Typical Family? Census Can't Say," *Boston Globe,* August 10, 1994.

[3] "What Is the Typical Family?"

[4] See Michel Foucault, *The History of Sexuality, Volume 1: An Introduction.* (New York: Random House, 1978); and John D'Emilio and Estelle Freedman, *Intimate Matters: A History of Sexuality in America* (New York: HarperCollins, 1988).

[5] John D'Emilio, "Capitalism and Gay Identity," in Ann Snitow, Christine Stansell, and Sharon Thompson, eds., *Powers of Desire: The Politics of Sexuality* (New York: Monthly Review Press, 1983), 100–116.

[6] Michelle Cuvilly Klopner and Loretta Saint-Louis, "Sexuality at a Crossroads: Haitian Immigrant Youth and Their Families" (unpublished manuscript).

[7] Deborah Lee and Kevin Fong, "HIV/AIDS and the Asian and Pacific Islander Community," *SIECUS Report* 18, no. 3 (1990): 16–22.

[8] Connie Chan, "Asian American Adolescents: Issues in the Expression of Sexuality," in Janice M. Irvine, ed., *Sexual Cultures and the Construction of Adolescent Identities* (Philadelphia: Temple University Press, 1994), 88–99.

[9] Lee and Fong.

[10] Coontz, 242.

• •

Epilogue

Multiculturalism requires a transformation of the curriculum. In sexuality education, this transformation involves a revolution in how we think about sexuality. Social construction theory has brought such a revolutionary perspective to the field of sexuality studies. It can help us to think about our own sex/gender systems and to evaluate our materials. It keeps us always focused on the possibility of difference and the likelihood of change, two elements that are central to multiculturalism.

Social Constructionism and Sexuality Education

A social constructionist approach to multicultural sexuality education is quite tangible and specific. First, we must be alert to the assumptions that underpin our lessons. Sexuality education materials, like all texts, carry implicit messages and values. This is true even when the lessons are about seemingly neutral topics like anatomy and physiology. If we are using packaged curricula, brochures, or videos, we can evaluate them for possible bias.

In particular, we want to avoid making universal assumptions about sexuality. The information we've covered in this book can help serve as a guide for asking a series of questions. For example, does the lesson appear to be aimed at only dominant groups such as European Americans and heterosexuals? Are there examples drawn from a range of cultural perspectives? Are pictures or illustrations effectively multicultural? Are some lessons, such as those concerning birth control or sexually transmitted diseases, illustrated predominantly with images of people of color? Are there assumptions about what activities and values constitute sexuality? If the material uses the term *sex* as a synonym for intercourse, for example, we will want to show our students how that illustrates a particular value about what counts the most as sex. We saw in Chapter Four that there were cultural differences in being sexual. We will want to correct material that makes assumptions about what it means to be a sexual person.

It is probably wise to assume that virtually all of our materials will contain some universalisms. As we discussed, even some of the most basic sex research, such as that by Alfred Kinsey and by William Masters and Virginia Johnson, was conducted on very narrow samples and then used as the basis for broad generalizations. If we teach the human sexual response cycle, we must remember that these so-called facts about sexual physiology were derived from a very biased sample made up of only middle-class European Americans. Sometimes, as in this case, there is no other study that corrects this bias. If we teach Masters and Johnson, however, we can tell our students how these researchers conducted their studies. It is certainly useful to teach students that examining the sample is one way in which to evaluate a study.

Second, we can take a historical approach to sexuality. This is an invaluable way to show how sexual values, attitudes, and practices can radically change. In Chapter Four we discussed teaching students about the historical invention of both homosexual and heterosexual identities. Abortion, birth control, pornography, adolescent sexuality, and prostitution are some other areas in which beliefs and behaviors have varied throughout the last one hundred years. These lessons don't have to be lengthy; often we have little enough time as it is. But even a five- or ten-minute discussion of historical changes can stimulate more expansive thinking. And historical lessons can support cross-cultural ones. We can more intuitively recognize cultural differences when we see how ideas about sexuality have changed, for example, that abortion was commonplace and noncontroversial in the dominant culture before the mid-nineteenth century or that the categories of heterosexual and homosexual are only one hundred years old.

Third, we want our students to see themselves in our lessons. Using a range of examples from different cultures can help accomplish this. Showing difference opens up the lesson to cultural diversity. We send an important message when we point out that a brochure addresses only heterosexuals or if we note that belief systems or behaviors may be different for European Americans, African Americans, or certain Latino groups. It is my belief that if we liberally sprinkle our lessons with diverse examples we have created a multicultural environment even if every single student's cultural group has not been specifically discussed.

Becoming Interculturally Competent

Sound multicultural sexuality education begins with each one of us. Our skills, motivation, and vision are the most important teaching tools we have. We don't need to be experts in multiculturalism. We can, however, enhance an intercultural competence that we can bring to our classrooms, workshop sessions, training groups, and individual counseling sessions.

We can learn these skills for more effective intercultural communication about sexuality. First, we must be prepared to acknowledge and confront our own discomfort and anxieties regarding difference. We live in a society divided by, and mistrustful of, difference. Many people grow up surrounded only by those who look like them and are taught to be suspicious of those who do not. These patterns are not easily broken. In addition to fears we may have about those who are different from us, we can also be afraid of saying or doing the wrong thing. Sometimes it feels easier to be silent than to risk being accused of racism or sexism.

It may be helpful to have a structured place, such as a support group, in which to deal with fears as well as racism, sexism, homophobia, and other destructive attitudes that all of us inevitably learn and internalize. Even talking regularly with a colleague or friend can be helpful. It is important, however, not to wait until we feel entirely comfortable before breaking the silence surrounding difference. We needn't be flawless. As John Noonan, director of the Center for Improving Teaching Effectiveness notes, "the image of the completely self-assured professional is archaic in a society filled with competing viewpoints."[1]

Second, knowledge of the patterns of one's own sex/gender system is vital. This is especially true for European Americans, who, as members of a dominant culture, can often experience their sexual perspectives and behaviors as universal. There are different routes to this self-awareness. Some educators may want to meet in discussion groups in which participants can examine the ways in which their own cultural backgrounds shaped their sexual worldviews. Some of the topics we've covered in this book—the role of the family, ways of being sexual, types of sexual language, and the influence of multiple identifications—can shape these discussions. Others may prefer to work individually, in which case a technique such as a retrospective journal might be helpful. It is only through a deep familiarity with our own sexual attitudes, beliefs, and behaviors that we can recognize differences and similarities with other cultures.

Third, some knowledge of the sex/gender systems of other cultures is essential. There is a growing literature on culture and sexuality (see Suggested Readings) that can be a resource. Many educators have little time for reading, but we can be open to learning through personal discussions and relationships, participation in diverse cultural events, and exposure to the popular media of other groups. Most of us read popular magazines, and it can be useful to subscribe to one that is targeted to a group different from our own.

Fourth, educators, especially those from dominant groups, must be aware of power inequities and the history of discrimination. This is especially true because we often enter groups seeking to change other people's behaviors. We want people to use a condom, practice birth control, or generally practice sex that is safer. Depending on cultural dynamics, this aim may well be met with indifference, anger, or resistance. Historically oppressed groups may be rightfully resentful of educators from outside their culture who approach them without an explicit sensitivity to dynamics of discrimination. White AIDS educators, for example, quickly learned that the Tuskegee experiments had fostered an understandable climate of suspicion and distrust that greeted their outreach efforts in African-American communities.

Fifth, the task of developing intercultural competence extends across cultures. All of us—not just individuals from dominant groups—must seek to enhance knowledge and respect for other cultures. For example, one sexuality educator from the United States described her shock when, at a training session, an African man explained to the Kenyan audience how Europeans sexualize women's breasts. By contrast, he pointed out, traditional Africans view the breast as a nonsexual body part. In making his point, he reached over and fondled her breasts, while she recoiled, stunned by his cultural insensitivity.[2]

Professionals from nondominant cultures can also be subjected to unrealistic expectations. They are often treated as experts on all other cultures. Yet it is a racist assumption to expect, for example, that African-American educators without multicultural training can easily work in Puerto Rican or Chinese communities simply because they are people of color. Again, the challenge to become more culturally competent extends to all of us.

Finally, personal commitment is crucial. In part, this means a willingness to challenge individuals and institutions that foster cultural ignorance and perpetuate social inequality. It isn't easy to speak out, and every moment isn't the right one to do so. But our multicultural efforts can't be confined to the classroom. We must challenge a school board that resists an inclusive curriculum or talk with a colleague who makes a racist remark. The commitment to multiculturalism is also a recognition of the importance of connection with those who are different from oneself. It entails openness, respect for others, empathy, flexibility, and readiness to risk the unpredictability of connection with others. This commitment is integral to effective intercultural communication, for as the literary critic Henry Louis Gates, Jr., notes, "No human culture is inaccessible to someone who makes the effort to understand, to learn, to inhabit another world."[3] As sexuality educators, our best work comes out of our efforts to inhabit our students' worlds, if only for a class session.

A Critical Approach to Diversity Training

It is increasingly common for schools or organizations to hire consultants for diversity training. This can be a productive step in moving a staff toward multicultural competency. Diversity consulting has become so common and so commercialized, however, that some critics have began to call it the "diversity industry." And, as in any industry, there are numerous products of differing quality. You will want to look carefully at the philosophies and techniques of consultants before you hire them.

If you are thinking about hiring diversity consultants, there are several points to consider. First, if you are particularly interested in culture and sexuality, be sure to ask if the consultants address this. It is a specialized area, and most diversity trainers do not specifically deal with sex/gender systems of different cultures.

Second, if the consultants address sexuality, ask about their theoretical approach to culture and sexuality. Ideally, they take a social constructionist approach. Avoid those who treat both culture and sexuality in static, simplistic ways. For example, we have seen the limitations of approaches that make sweeping generalizations about sexuality in different racial and ethnic groups.

Third, ask consultants whether their focus is on either the individual or the institution. There is a strain of diversity training, for example, in which individual prejudice is the focal point of the program. Consultants of this "school" work on an emotional, counseling level with members of an organization in an attempt to heal old wounds from discrimination. You can recognize these programs by the buzzwords *prejudice reduction.* At the other extreme are programs geared solely toward managerial concerns. These are probably inappropriate for the goals of educators and social service professionals. Buzzwords of these programs are *managing diversity* and *legal compliance.* Ideally, you want consultants who can address such individual concerns as fear and anger. But it is crucial to move beyond the individual level and be able to recognize how, in our society, differences usually translate into inequalities. We want to work to free ourselves of prejudice, but we also want to examine how our schools or agencies might reinforce inequality through certain policies or curricula.

Bringing in a consultant can be a great idea, but it is well worth doing some research so that you make a sound choice. I have seen the staff at many workplaces end up sorely disappointed, and even angry, because a diversity trainer's approach proved to be way off base.

Before interviewing consultants, you may want to do some reading about diversity trainers. DeRosa and Mohanty have authored useful articles; both discuss the "diversity industry," and DeRosa lays out a useful schema of the common philosophies of six different methods.[1]

[1] Patti DeRosa, "Diversity Training: In Search of Anti-Racism," *Peacework: Global Thought and Local Action for Nonviolent Social Change,* no. 240 (April 1994); Chandra Talpade Mohanty, "On Race and Voice: Challenges for Liberal Education in the 1990s," in Henry Giroux and Peter McLaren, eds., *Between Borders: Pedagogy and the Politics of Cultural Studies* (New York: Routledge & Kegan Paul, 1994), 145–166.

References

Preface

1. Debra Haffner, *Sex Education 2000: A Call to Action*. (New York: Sex Information and Education Council of the United States [SIECUS], 1990).

2. James A. Banks, *Teaching Strategies for Ethnic Studies*, 5th ed. (Needham Heights, Mass.: Allyn & Bacon, 1991).

3. Janie Ward and Jill Taylor, "Sexuality Education for Immigrant and Minority Students," in Janice M. Irvine, ed., *Sexual Cultures and the Construction of Adolescent Identities* (Philadelphia: Temple University Press, 1994), 51–68.

4. See Merrill Singer, "Confronting the AIDS Epidemic Among IV Drug Users: Does Ethnic Culture Matter?" *AIDS Education and Prevention* 3, no. 3 (1991): 258–283; M. Agar, "Toward an Ethnographic Language," *American Anthropologist* 84 (1982): 779–795.

Chapter One

1. Herman N. Bundesen, *Toward Manhood* (Philadelphia: Lippincott, 1951), quoted in Patricia J. Campbell, *Sex Education Books for Young Adults 1892–1979* (New York: R. R. Bowker, 1979), 102.

2. Bryan Strong and Christine DeVault, *Human Sexuality* (Mountain View, Calif.: Mayfield, 1994), 734.

3. D. A. Read and W. H. Greene, *Creative Teaching in Health*, quoted in Mariamne H. Whatley, "Male and Female Hormones: Misinterpretations of Biology in School Health and Sex Education," in

V. Sapiro, ed., *Women, Biology, and Public Policy* (Newbury Park: Calif.: Sage, 1985).

4. Sr. Jeannine Gramick, "Homosexuality and Bisexuality Are Just as Natural and Normal as Heterosexual Behavior and Relations," in Robert T. Francoeur, ed., *Taking Sides: Clashing Views on Controversial Issues in Human Sexuality* (Guilford, Conn.: Dushkin, 1987), 73–74.

5. Leslie Holliday, "Values in a Decade of Decision" (unpublished paper, 1993, Newton, Mass.).

6. Herman N. Bundesen, op. cit.

7. Letter to the editor, *Boston Globe*, May 30, 1994.

8. Janice M. Irvine, "Regulated Passions: The Invention of Inhibited Sexual Desire and Sex Addiction," *Social Text* 37 (Winter 1993): 203–226.

9. Gayle Rubin, "The Traffic in Women: Notes on the 'Political Economy' of Sex," in Rayna R. Reiter, ed., *Toward an Anthropology of Women* (New York: Monthly Review Press, 1975).

10. Strong and DeVault, 24.

11. Gilbert Herdt, *Guardians of the Flutes: Idioms of Masculinity* (New York: McGraw-Hill, 1981).

12. See Carole S. Vance, "Anthropology Rediscovers Sexuality: A Theoretical Comment," *Social Science and Medicine* 33, no. 8 (1991): 875–884; Leonore Tiefer, *Sex Is Not a Natural Act & Other Essays* (Boulder, Colo.: Westview Press, 1995).

13. See Janice M. Irvine, "From Difference to Sameness: Gender Ideology in Sexual Science," *Journal of Sex Research* 27, no. 1 (February 1990): 7–24; Cynthia E. Russett, *Sexual Science* (Cambridge, Mass.: Harvard University Press, 1989); Jeffrey Weeks, *Sex, Politics, and Society: The Regulation of Sexuality Since 1800* (White Plains, N.Y.: Longman, 1981).

14. Janice M. Irvine, *Disorders of Desire: Sex and Gender in Modern American Sexology* (Philadelphia: Temple University Press, 1990).

15. See Edward Laumann, John Gagnon, Robert Michael, and Stuart Michaels, *The Social Organization of Sexuality: Sexual Practices in the United States* (Chicago: University of Chicago Press: 1994).

16. See Mariamne H. Whatley, "Male and Female Hormones: Misinterpretations of Biology in School Health and Sex Education," in V. Sapiro, ed., *Women, Biology, and Public Policy* (Newbury Park: Calif.: Sage, 1985).

Chapter Two

1. George R. Saunders, "Men and Women in Southern Europe: A Review of Some Aspects of Cultural Complexity," *Journal of Psychoanalytic Anthropology* 4, no. 4 (1981): 434–466.

2. John L. Peterson, "Black Men and Their Same-Sex Desires and Behaviors," in Gilbert H. Herdt, ed., *Gay Culture in America: Essays from the Field* (Boston: Beacon Press, 1992), 147–164.

3. Kimberle Crenshaw, "Whose Story Is It Anyway? Feminist and Antiracist Appropriations of Anita Hill," in Toni Morrison, ed., *Race-ing Justice, En-gendering Power: Essays on Anita Hill, Clarence Thomas, and the Construction of Social Reality* (New York: Pantheon, 1992), 402–440.

4. Stuart Hall, "Ethnicity: Identity and Difference," *Radical America* 23, no. 4 (1989).

5. Mariamne H. Whatley, "Keeping Adolescents in the Picture: Construction of Adolescent Sexuality in Textbook Images and Popular Films," in Irvine, *Sexual Cultures*, 183–205.

6. Ruth Frankenberg, *White Women, Race Matters: The Social Construction of Whiteness* (Minneapolis: University of Minnesota Press, 1993).

7. Jeffrey Weeks, *Against Nature: Essays on History, Sexuality, and Identity* (London: Rivers Oram Press, 1991), viii.

8. William Simon and John H. Gagnon, "Sexual Scripts: Permanence and Change," *Archives of Sexual Behavior* 15, no. 2 (1986): 97–120; see also Laumann, Gagnon, Michael, and Michaels.

9. Excerpts from the ABC series "My So-Called Life," Episode #59404 "Pressure" written by Ellen Herman, are used with permission. © 1994 a.k.a. Productions, Inc.

10. Excerpts from the ABC series "My So-Called Life," Episode #59404 "Pressure" written by Ellen Herman, are used with permission. © 1994 a.k.a. Productions, Inc.

11. Sol Gordon, *You Would If You Loved Me* (New York: Bantam Books, 1978).

12. *Talking with Your Partner About Using Condoms* (brochure produced by ETR Associates, 1989).

13. Excerpts from the ABC series "My So-Called Life," Episode #59404 "Pressure" written by Ellen Herman, are used with permission. © 1994 a.k.a. Productions, Inc.

14. See Janet R. Kahn, "Speaking Across Cultures Within Your Own Family," in Irvine, *Sexual Cultures*, 285–309; Ward and Taylor, 51–70.

15. Aanitra Pivnick, "HIV Infection and the Meaning of Condoms," *Culture, Medicine, and Psychiatry* (December 1993): 431–453.

Chapter Three

1. See, for example, Michael Omi and Howard Winant, *Racial Formations in the United States: From the 1960s to the 1980s* (New York: Routledge & Kegan Paul, 1986); Howard Winant, *Racial Conditions* (Minneapolis: University of Minnesota Press, 1994).

2. James Shreeve, "Terms of Estrangement," *Discover* (November 1994): 57–60.

3. See Richard Lewontin, *Human Diversity* (New York: Scientific American Books, 1982).

4. Omi and Winant, 68.

5. Richard J. Herrnstein and Charles Murray, *The Bell Curve*. (New York: The Free Press, 1994).

6. Lawrence Wright, "One Drop of Blood," *New Yorker*, July 25, 1994, 46–55.

7. Reginald McKnight, "Confessions of a Wannabe Negro," in Gerald Early, ed., *Lure and Loathing: Essays on Race, Identity, and the Ambivalence of Assimilation* (New York: Penguin, 1993).

8. Stephen L. Carter, "The Black Table, the Empty Seat, and the Tie," in Early, *Lure and Loathing*.

9. Shirlee Taylor Haizlip, *The Sweeter the Juice: A Family Memoir in Black and White* (New York: Simon and Schuster, 1994), 266.

10. Winthrop Jordan, "First Impressions: Libidinous Blacks," in Ronald Takaki, ed., *From Different Shores: Perspectives on Race and Ethnicity in America* (New York: Oxford University Press, 1994), 47.

11. Ronald Takaki, *A Different Mirror: A History of Multicultural America* (Boston: Little, Brown, 1993).

12. Takaki, *A Different Mirror*, 39.

13. John D'Emilio and Estelle Freedman, *Intimate Matters: A History of Sexuality in America* (New York: HarperCollins, 1988).

14. D'Emilio and Freedman, 7.

15. D'Emilio and Freedman, 88.

16. Takaki, *A Different Mirror*, 148–149.

17. D'Emilio and Freedman, 107.

18. Jacquelyn Dowd Hall, "'The Mind That Burns in Each Body': Women, Rape, and Racial Violence," in Ann Snitow, Christine Stansell, and Sharon Thompson, eds., *Powers of Desire: The Politics of Sexuality* (New York: Monthly Review Press, 1983), 328–349.

19. Gail E. Wyatt, "The Sociocultural Context of African American and White American Women's Rape," *Journal of Social Issues* 48, no. 1 (1992): 77–91.

20. Maulana Karenga, "Under the Camouflage of Color and Gender: The Dread and Drama of Thomas-Hill," in R. Chrisman and R. Allen, eds , *Court of Appeal* (New York: Ballantine, 1992)

21. Pamela M. Wilson, "Black Culture and Sexuality," *Journal of Social Work and Human Sexuality* 4, no. 3 (1986): 29–46.

22. Katherine A. Forrest and others, "Exploring Norms and Beliefs Related to AIDS Prevention Among California Hispanic Men," *Family Planning Perspectives* 25, no. 3 (May–June 1993): 115.

23. Whatley, "Keeping Adolescents in the Picture," 183–205.

Chapter Four

1. Cindy Patton, "Resistance and the Erotic: Reclaiming History, Setting Strategy as We Face AIDS," *Radical America* 20, no. 6 (1986): 68–74.

2. D'Emilio and Freedman.

3. Arline T. Geronimus, "On Teenage Childbearing and Neonatal Mortality in the United States," *Population and Development Review* 13, no. 2 (1987): 245–279.

4. Geronimus.

5. Kristin Luker, "Dubious Conceptions: The Controversy over Teen Pregnancy," *American Prospect* (Spring 1991): 73–83.

6. Geronimus.

7. Geronimus; see also Carol Stack, *All Our Kin* (New York: HarperCollins, 1974).

8. Michael A. Carrera, "Involving Adolescent Males in Pregnancy and STD Prevention Programs," *Adolescent Medicine* 3, no. 2 (June 1992).

9. Michael A. Carrera and others, "Evaluating a Comprehensive Pregnancy Prevention Program," *FLEducator* (Fall 1992): 6.

10. Gilbert Herdt, *Guardians of the Flutes* (New York: McGraw-Hill, 1981).

11. Alfred C. Kinsey, Wardell B. Pomeroy, Clyde E. Martin, and Paul H. Gebhard, *Sexual Behavior in the Human Male* (Philadelphia: Saunders, 1948), 393.

12. Laumann, Gagnon, Michael, and Michaels.

13. Martin Weinberg and Colin Williams, "Black Sexuality: A Test of Two Theories," *Journal of Sex Research* 25, no. 2 (1988): 197–218.

14. See Weinberg and Williams for a review of much of this research; see also Laumann, Gagnon, Michael, and Michaels.

15. Gail E. Wyatt and others, "Kinsey Revisited, Part II: Comparisons of the Sexual Socialization and Sexual Behavior of Black Women over 33 Years," *Archives of Sexual Behavior* 17, no. 4 (1988): 289–332; see also Laumann, Gagnon, Michael, and Michaels.

16. Weinberg and Williams; Philip Belcastro, "Sexual Behavior Differences Between Black and White Students," *Journal of Sex Research* 21, no. 1 (1985): 56–67; see also Laumann, Gagnon, Michael, and Michaels.

17. Gail E. Wyatt, "Ethnic and Cultural Differences in Women's Sexual Behavior," in Susan Blumenthal, Anita Eichler, and Gloria Weissman, eds., *Women and AIDS: Promoting Healthy Behavior* (New Brunswick, N.J.: Rutgers University Press, in press); see also Laumann, Gagnon, Michael, and Michaels.

18. Weinberg and Williams; see also Laumann, Gagnon, Michael, and Michaels.

19. Gail E. Wyatt, "Examining Predictors of Sex Guilt in Multiethnic Samples of Women," *Archives of Sexual Behavior* 20, no. 5 (1991): 471–485.

20. Mindy Thompson Fullilove and others, "Race/Gender Issues in the Sexual Transmission of AIDS," in Paul Volberding and Mark Jacobson, eds., *AIDS Clinical Review 1990* (New York: Marcel Dekker, 1990).

21. Wilson, 29–46.

22. Fullilove and others, 36.

23. Kinsey, Pomeroy, Martin, and Gebhard, 329.

24. National Guidelines Task Force, *Guidelines for Comprehensive Sexuality Education*. (New York: SIECUS, 1991).

25. D'Emilio and Freedman.

26. Michel Foucault, *The History of Sexuality, Volume 1: An Introduction*. (New York: Random House, 1978); Jeffrey Weeks, *Coming*

Out: Homosexual Politics in Britain, from the Nineteenth Century to the Present (London: Quartet Books, 1977).

27. Jonathan Katz, "The Invention of Heterosexuality," *Socialist Review*, no. 21 (1990): 7–34.

28. Kinsey, Pomeroy, Martin, and Gebhard, 639.

29. Tomas Almaguer, "Chicano Men: A Cartography of Homosexual Identity and Behavior," *differences* 3, no. 2 (1991): 75–100; and Ernesto de la Vega, "Considerations for Reaching the Latino Population with Sexuality and HIV/AIDS Information and Education," *SIECUS Report* 18, no. 3 (1990): 1–8.

30. The Michigan Lesbian Health Survey, MOHR (Michigan Organization for Human Rights) Special Report, August 1991.

31. Joyce Hunter and others, "Sexual and Substance Abuse Acts That Place Adolescent Lesbians at Risk for HIV" (Poster presented at the Ninth International Conference on AIDS/HIV STD World Congress, Berlin, Germany, 7–11 June 1993).

32. Weeks, *Against Nature*, viii.

33. Albert Klassen, Colin Williams, and Eugene Levitt, *Sex and Morality in the U.S.* (Middletown, Conn.: Wesleyan University Press, 1989).

34. Harlan Dalton, "AIDS in Blackface," *Positively Aware* (February 1992): 23.

35. John Peterson, "Black Men and Their Same-Sex Desires and Behaviors," in Gilbert Herdt, ed., *Gay Culture in America: Essays from the Field* (Boston: Beacon Press, 1992), 147–164.

36. Dalton, 25.

37. Dalton, 23; bell hooks, "Homophobia in Black Communities," *Zeta* 1 (March 1988): 35–38.

38. Alan P. Bell and Martin S. Weinberg, *Homosexualities: A Study of Diversity Among Men and Women* (New York: Simon and Schuster, 1978).

39. Gloria Anzaldúa, *Borderlands: La Frontera* (San Francisco: Aunt Lute Books, 1987).

40. Almaguer.

41. Almaguer.

42. Cherrie Moraga, quoted in Almaguer, 92.

43. Almaguer, 77.

44. Almaguer.

45. Cherrie Moraga, *Loving in the War Years* (Boston: South End Press, 1983).

Chapter 5

1. See Barrie Thorne, *Gender Play: Girls and Boys in School* (New Brunswick, N.J.: Rutgers University Press, 1993) for a view that gender should not be considered a culture; see also "On In a Different Voice: An Interdisciplinary Forum," *Signs: Journal of Women in Culture and Society*, 11, No. 2, (1986).

2. Bernie Zilbergeld, *The New Male Sexuality: A Guide to Sexual Fulfillment* (Boston: Little, Brown, 1992).

3. Reiko True, "Psychotherapeutic Issues with Asian American Women," *Sex Roles* 22, nos. 7–8 (1990): 477–486.

4. Forrest and others, 111–117.

5. See Toni Morrison, ed., *Race-ing Justice, En-gendering Power: Essays on Anita Hill, Clarence Thomas, and the Construction of Social Reality* (New York: Pantheon, 1992).

6. Charles Leerhsen, "Ann Landers and 'the Act,'" *Newsweek*, January 28, 1985.

7. Mariamne Whatley, "Raging Hormones and Powerful Cars: The Construction of Men's Sexuality in School Sex Education and Popular Adolescent Films," *Journal of Education* 170, no. 3 (1988): 100–121.

8. See, for example, Gail Vines, *Raging Hormones: Do They Rule Our Lives?* (Berkeley: University of California Press, 1994); Ruth Hubbard and Elijah Wald, *Exploding the Gene Myth* (Boston: Beacon Press, 1993).

9. Lillian Rubin, *Worlds of Pain: Life in the Working-Class Family* (New York: Basic Books, 1976).

10. S. Hofferth and C. Hayes, eds., *Risking the Future: Adolescent Sexuality, Pregnancy, and Childbearing,* vol. 2 (Washington, D.C.: National Academy Press, 1987).

11. Diane Raymond, "Homophobia, Identity, and the Meanings of Desire: Reflections on the Cultural Construction of Gay and Lesbian Adolescent Sexuality," in Irvine, *Sexual Cultures,* 115–150.

12. Kinsey, Pomeroy, Martin, and Gebhard, *Sexual Behavior in the Human Male;* Alfred C. Kinsey, Wardell B. Pomeroy, Clyde E. Martin, and Paul H. Gebhard, *Sexual Behavior in the Human Female* (New York: Pocket Books, 1953).

13. Irvine, *Disorders of Desire.*

14. Weinberg and Williams, 197–218.

15. Laumann, Gagnon, Michael, and Michaels.

16. Kahn, 285–309.

17. Elijah Anderson, *Street Wise: Race, Class, and Change in an Urban Community* (Chicago: University of Chicago Press, 1990).

18. Anderson, 114.

19. Anderson, 118.

20. Anderson, 117.

21. Sharon Thompson, "'Drastic Entertainments': Teenage Mothers' Signifying Narratives," in Faye Ginsburg and Anna Tsing, eds., *Uncertain Terms: Negotiating Gender in American Culture* (Boston: Beacon Press, 1990), 269–281.

22. Thompson, 274.

23. Carl Degler, "What Ought to Be and What Was: Women's Sexuality in the Nineteenth Century," in Judith Walzer Leavitt, ed., *Women and Health in America* (Madison: University of Wisconsin Press, 1984), 40–56.

24. Nancy Cott, "Passionlessness: An Interpretation of Victorian Sexual Ideology, 1790–1850," in Leavitt, 57–69.

25. See Irvine, "Regulated Passions"; D'Emilio and Freedman.

26. See Irvine, "Regulated Passions," 203–226.

27. Michelle Fine, "Sexuality, Schooling, and Adolescent Females: The Missing Discourse of Desire," *Harvard Educational Review* 58, no. 1 (1988): 29–53.

28. D'Emilio and Freedman.

29. Deborah Tolman, "Daring to Desire: Culture and the Bodies of Adolescent Girls," in Irvine, *Sexual Cultures*, 250–284.

30. Raymond, 141.

31. See Margaret Nichols, "Low Sexual Desire in Lesbian Couples," in Sandra Leiblum and Raymond Rosen, eds., *Sexual Desire Disorders* (New York: Guilford Press, 1988), 387–412; Philip Blumstein and Pepper Schwartz, *American Couples: Money, Work, and Sex* (New York: Morrow, 1983).

32. Carole S. Vance, ed., *Pleasure and Danger: Exploring Female Sexuality* (London: Pandora, 1992).

33. Vance, *Pleasure and Danger: Exploring Female Sexuality*, 4.

34. See, for example, Rubin; Maxine Baca Zinn, "Chicano Men and Masculinity," *Journal of Ethnic Studies* 10, no. 2: 29–44; V. L. Cromwell and R. E. Cromwell, "Perceived Dominance in Decision-Making and Conflict Resolution Among Anglo, Black, and Chicano Couples," *Journal of Marriage and Family* 40 (1978): 749–759.

35. Irvine, *Disorders of Desire*.

36. Michael Miller, "Variations in Mexican-American Family Life," quoted in Baca Zinn, p. 29.

37. Baca Zinn.

38. Anne Kline, Emily Kline, and Emily Oken, "Minority Women and Sexual Choice in the Age of AIDS," *Social Science and Medicine* 34, no. 4 (1992): 447–457.

39. Kline, Kline, and Oken.

40. Kline, Kline, and Oken, 451.

41. Kline, Kline, and Oken, 453

42. Cromwell and Cromwell.

Chapter Six

1. Ethan Bronner, "Translating the Politics of Reproduction," *Boston Globe*, September 9, 1994.

2. Irvine, *Disorders of Desire*.

3. E. H. Hare, "Masturbatory Insanity: The History of an Idea," *Journal of Mental Science* 108, no. 452 (1962): 2–25.

4. Elizabeth Lunbeck, "'A New Genderation of Women': Progressive Psychiatrists and the Hypersexual Female," *Feminist Studies* 13, no. 3 (1987): 513–543.

5. Irvine, *Disorders of Desire*.

6. Janice M. Irvine, "Reinventing Perversion: Sex Addiction and Cultural Anxieties," *Journal of the History of Sexuality* (January 1995).

7. D'Emilio and Freedman.

8. Janet Sanders and William Robinson, "Talking and Not Talking About Sex: Male and Female Vocabularies," *Journal of Communication* 29, no. 2 (1979): 22–30.

9. Sandra Mondykowski, "Polish Families," in Monica McGoldrick, John Pearce, and Joseph Giordano, eds., *Ethnicity and Family Therapy* (New York: Guilford Press, 1982), 393–411.

10. Mindy Fullilove and others, "Black Women and AIDS Prevention: Understanding the Gender Rules," *Journal of Sex Research* 27, no. 1 (1990): 47–64.

11. Gloria Joseph and Jill Lewis, *Common Differences: Conflicts in Black and White Feminist Perspectives* (Boston: South End Press, 1981).

12. Wright, 46–55.

13. See Ernesto de la Vega, "Considerations for Reaching the Latino Population with Sexuality and HIV/AIDS Information and Education," *SIECUS Report* 13, no. 3 (1990): 1–8.

14. Forrest and others, 111–117.

15. de la Vega.

16. Deborah Tannen, *Gender & Discourse* (New York: Oxford University Press, 1994), 71–72.

17. Deborah Tannen, *You Just Don't Understand: Women and Men in Conversation* (New York: Ballantine, 1990).

18. Tannen, *You Just Don't Understand*, 88.

19. Tannen, *Gender & Discourse*.

20. Tannen, *Gender & Discourse*; see also Nikolas Coupland, Howard Giles, and John Wiemann, eds., *"Miscommunication" and Problematic Talk* (Newbury Park, Calif.: Sage, 1991).

21. Kahn, 285–309.

Chapter Seven

1. Hilary Homans and Peter Aggleton, "Health Education, HIV Infection and AIDS," in Peter Aggleton and Hilary Homans, eds., *Social Aspects of AIDS* (London: Falmer Press, 1988), 154–176.

2. Marshall H. Becker, "The Health Belief Model and Personal Health Behavior," *Health Education Monograph* 2 (1974): 324–508; I. M. Rosenstock, "Historical Origins of the Health Belief Model," *Health Education Monograph* 2 (1974).

3. See Nancy Janz and Marshall Becker, "The Health Belief Model: A Decade Later," *Health Education Quarterly* 11, no. 1 (1984): 1–47.

4. Jill G. Joseph and others, "Magnitude and Determinants of Behavioral Risk Reduction: Longitudinal Analysis of a Cohort at Risk for AIDS," *Psychology and Health* 1 (1987): 73–96.

5. Joy Dryfoos, *Adolescents at Risk: Prevalence and Prevention* (New York: Oxford University Press, 1990).

6. Dryfoos.

7. Kristin Luker, *Taking Chances: Abortion and the Decision Not to Contracept* (Berkeley: University of California Press, 1975), 49.

8. Luker, 70.

9. Rosalind P. Petchesky, *Abortion and Woman's Choice: The State, Sexuality, and Reproductive Freedom* (White Plains, N.Y.: Longman, 1984).

10. See Sharon Thompson, "Search for Tomorrow: Feminism and the Reconstruction of Teen Romance," in Vance, *Pleasure and Danger*,

350–384; Sharon Thompson, *Going All the Way* (New York: Farrar, Straus & Giroux, 1995).

11. Petchesky, 223.

12. E. J. Sobo, "Inner-City Woman and AIDS: The Psycho-Social Benefits of Unsafe Sex," *Culture, Medicine, and Psychiatry* (December 1993): 455–485.

13. Isabelle De Vincenzi, "A Longitudinal Study of Human Immuno-deficiency Virus Transmission by Heterosexual Partners," *The New England Journal of Medicine* 331, no. 6 (August 11, 1994).

14. Ian Warwick, Peter Aggleton, and Hilary Homans, "Young People's Health Beliefs and AIDS," in Aggleton and Homans, 106–125.

15. Pivnick, 431–453.

16. See, for example, Dalton, 205–227.

17. Sobo.

18. Sobo.

19. Sobo, 467; see also Dalton.

20. Sobo.

21. Pivnick, 444.

22. See Pivnick.

23. For different opinions see Sobo; Pivnick; Anne Kline, Emily Kline and Emily Oken, 447–457.

24. Sobo.

25. Sobo, 478.

26. Vincent Covello and Branden Johnson, "The Social and Cultural Construction of Risk: Issues, Methods, and Case Studies," in B. B. Johnson and V. T. Covello, eds., *The Social and Cultural Construction of Risk* (Dordrecht, Netherlands: D. Reidel, 1987), viii.

27. Robert Bullard, *Dumping in Dixie: Race, Class, and Environmental Quality* (Boulder, Colo.: Westview Press, 1994).

28. Charles Radin, "AIDS Fight Portrayed as a Failure," *Boston Globe*, August 10, 1994, 10.

Chapter Eight

1. John Noonan, "Discussing Racial Topics in Class" (unpublished paper, November 1982, Virginia Commonwealth University).

2. Nanette Ecker, "Culture and Sexual Scripts Out of Africa," *SIECUS Report* (December 1993–January 1994): 16–21.

3. Henry Louis Gates, Jr., "'Authenticity,' or the Lesson of Little Tree," *New York Times Book Review*, November 24, 1991.

Additional Readings

Ahn, H. N., and Gilbert, N. "Cultural Diversity and Sexual Abuse Prevention." *Social Service Review*, Sept. 1992, 66(3), 410–428.

Airhihenbuwa, C., DeClemente, R., Wingood, G., and Lowe, A. "HIV/AIDS Education and Prevention Among African-Americans: A Focus on Culture." *AIDS Education and Prevention*, 1992, 4(3), 267–276.

Amaro, H. "Considerations for Prevention of HIV Infection Among Hispanic Women." *Psychology of Women Quarterly*, 1988, 12, 429–443.

Aneshensel, C., Fielder, E., and Becerra, R. "Fertility and Fertility-Related Behavior Among Mexican-American and Non-Hispanic White Females." *Journal of Health and Social Behavior*, Mar. 1989, 30(1), 56–78.

Baldwin, J. D., Whiteley, S., and Baldwin, J. I. "The Effect of Ethnic Group on Sexual Activities Related to Contraception and STDs." *Journal of Sex Research*, May 1992, 29(2), 189–206.

Banks, I. W., and Wilson, P. I. "Appropriate Sex Education for Black Teens." *Adolescence*, Spring 1989, 24, 233–245.

Bean, F., and Tienda, M. *The Hispanic Population of the United States*. New York: Russell Sage Foundation, 1987.

Becerra, R. "The Mexican American Family." In C. H. Mindel, R. W. Habenstein, and R. Wright, Jr.(eds.), *Ethnic Families in America: Patterns and Variations*. (3rd ed.) New York: Elsevier North Holland, 1988.

Billy, J., Tanfer, K., Grady, W. R., and Klepinger, D. H. "The Sexual Behavior of Men in the United States." *Family Planning Perspectives*, Mar. 1993, 25(2), 52–60.

Binion, V. "Psychological Androgyny: A Black Female Perspective." *Sex Roles*, April 1990, 22, 7–8.

Blackwood, E. "Sexuality and Gender in Certain Native American Tribes: The Case of Cross-Gender Females." *Signs: A Journal of Women in Culture and Society*, 1984, 10, 27–42.

Boles, J. J., and Curtis-Boles, H. "Black Couples and the Transition to Parenthood." *American Journal of Social Psychiatry*, Dec. 1986, 6(1), 27–31.

Bond, S., and Cash, T. F. "Black Beauty—Skin Color and Body Images Among African-American College Women." *Journal of Applied Social Psychology*, 1992, 22(11), 874–888.

Bonilla, L., and Porter, J. "A Comparison of Latino, Black, and Non-Hispanic White Attitudes Toward Homosexuality." *Hispanic Journal of Behavioral Sciences*, 1990, 12, 437–452.

Bowser, B. P., Fullilove, M. T., and Fullilove, R. E. "African-American Youth and AIDS High-Risk Behavior: The Social Context and Barriers to Prevention." *Youth and Society*, Sept. 1990, 22(1), 54–66.

Brown, J. D., and Campbell, K. "Race and Gender in Music Videos: The Same Beat but a Different Drummer." *Journal of Communication*, Dec. 1986, 36(1), 94–106.

Brown, J. D., and Schulze, L. "The Effects of Race, Gender, and Fandom on Audience Interpretations of Madonna's Music Videos." *Journal of Communication*, 1990, 40, 88–102.

Bryant, Z. L., and Coleman, M. "The Black Family as Portrayed in Introductory Marriage and Family Textbooks." *Family Relations*, July 1988, 37(3), 255–259.

Butts, J. D. "Adolescent Sexuality and Teenage Pregnancy from a Black Perspective." In T. Ooms (ed.), *Teenage Pregnancy in a Family Context*. Philadelphia: Temple University Press, 1981.

Callender, C., and others. "The North American Berdache." *Current Anthropology*, Aug. 1983, 24(4), 443–456.

Campbell, P. J. *Sex Education Books for Young Adults 1892–1979*. New York: R. R. Bowker, 1979.

Caplan, A. L. "Twenty Years After. The Legacy of the Tuskegee Syphilis Study. When Evil Intrudes." *Hastings Center Report*, Nov. 1992, 22(6), 29–32.

Carlson, R. G., and Siegal, H. A. "The Crack Life: An Ethnographic Overview of Crack Use and Sexual Behavior Among African-Americans in a Midwest Metropolitan City." *Journal of Psychoactive Drugs*, Jan./Mar. 1991, 23(1), 11–20.

Carovano, K. "More Than Mothers and Whores: Redefining the AIDS Prevention Needs of Women." *International Journal of Health Services*, 1991, 21(1), 131–142.

Carrier, J. "Miguel: Sexual Life History of a Gay Mexican American." In G. Herdt (ed.), *Gay Culture in America: Essays from the Field*. Boston: Beacon Press, 1992.

Carrier, J., Joseph, B., and Nguyen, S. "Vietnamese American Sexual Behaviors and the HIV Infection." *Journal of Sex Research*, Nov. 1992, *29*(4), 547–560.

Carrier, J., and Magana, J. R. "Use of Ethnosexual Data on Men of Mexican Origin for HIV/AIDS Prevention Programs." *The Journal of Sex Research*, May 1991, *28*(2), 189–202.

Chapman, A. "Male-Female Relations: How the Past Affects the Present." In H. McAdoo (ed.), *Black Families*. (2nd ed.) Newbury Park, Calif.: Sage, 1988.

Cochran, S. D., Mays, V. M., and Leung, L. "Sexual Practices of Heterosexual Asian-American Young Adults: Implications for Risk of HIV Infection." *Archives of Sexual Behavior*, Aug. 1991, *20*(4), 381–394.

Collier, M. J. "Conflict Competence Within African, Mexican, and Anglo American Friendships." In S. Ting-Toomey and F. Korzenny (eds.), *Cross-Cultural Interpersonal Communication*. Newbury Park, Calif.: Sage, 1991.

Cortese, A. "Subcultural Differences in Human Sexuality: Race, Ethnicity, and Social Class." In K. McKinney and S. Sprecher (eds.), *Human Sexuality: The Societal and Interpersonal Context*. Norwood, N.J.: Ablex, 1989.

Crawford, I., and others. "Attitudes of African-American Baptist Ministers Toward AIDS." *Journal of Community Psychology*, 1992, *20*(4), 304–308.

DeCosta-Willis, M., and others (eds.). *Erotique Noire/Black Erotica*. New York: Doubleday, 1992.

DelCarmen, R. "Assessment of Asian-Americans for Family Therapy." In F. Serafica and others (eds.), *Mental Health of Ethnic Minorities*. New York: Praeger, 1990.

Demb, J. M. "Abortion in Inner-City Adolescents: What the Girls Say." *Family Systems Medicine*, 1991, *9*, 93–102.

Dorfman, L. E., Derish, P. A., and Cohen, J. B. "Hey Girlfriend: An Evaluation of AIDS Prevention Among Women in the Sex Industry." *Health Education Quarterly*, Spring 1992, pp. 25–40.

Drugger, K. "Social Location and Gender-Role Attitudes: A Comparison of Black and White Women." *Gender and Society*, Dec. 1988, *2*(4), 425–448.

DuRant, R., Pendergast, R., and Seymore, C. "Contraceptive Behavior Among Sexually Active Hispanic Adolescents." *Journal of Adolescent Health*, Nov. 1990, *11*(6), 490–496.

Ernst, F., and others. "Condemnation of Homosexuality in the Black Community: A Gender-Specific Phenomenon?" *Archives of Sexual Behavior*, 1991, *20*(6), 579–585.

Espin, O. M. "Cultural and Historical Influences on Sexuality in Hispanic/Latin Women: Implications for Psychotherapy." In C. S. Vance (ed.), *Pleasure and Danger: Exploring Female Sexuality*. New York: Routledge & Kegan Paul, 1984.

Falicov, C. "Mexican Families." In M. McGoldrick, J. K. Pearce, and J. Giordano (eds.), *Ethnicity and Family Therapy*. New York: Guilford Press, 1982.

Fossett, M. A., and Kiecolt, K. J. "Mate Availability and Family Structure Among African Americans in Metropolitan Areas." *Journal of Marriage and the Family*, 1993, *55*(2), 288–302.

Franklin, D. L. "The Impact of Early Childbearing on Developmental Outcomes: The Case of Black Adolescent Parenting." *Family Relations*, 1988, *37*, 268–274.

Furstenberg, F. F. "Race Differences in Teenage Sexuality, Pregnancy, and Adolescent Childbearing." *Milbank Quarterly*, 1987, *65*(Suppl. 2), 381–403.

Gibson, J., and Dempf, J. "Attitudinal Predictors of Sexual Activity in Hispanic Adolescent Females." *Journal of Adolescent Research*, 1990, *5*(4), 414–430.

Griswold Del Castillo, R. *La Familia: Chicano Families in the Urban Southwest, 1848 to the Present*. Notre Dame, Ind.: University of Notre Dame, 1984.

Guerrero Pavich, E. "A Chicana Perspective on Mexican Culture and Sexuality." In L. Lister (ed.), *Human Sexuality, Ethnoculture, and Social Work*. New York: Haworth Press, 1986.

hooks, b. "Homophobia in Black Communities," *Zeta*, March 1988, *1*.

Howard, J. "A Structural Approach to Interracial Patterns in Adolescent Judgments About Sexual Intimacy." *Sociological Perspectives*, Jan. 1988, *31*(1), 88–121.

Jemmott, J. B., Jemmott, L. S., and Fong, G. T. "Reductions in HIV Risk-Associated Sexual Behaviors Among Black Male Adolescents: Effects of an AIDS Prevention Intervention." *American Journal of Public Health*, March 1992, *82*(3), 372–377.

Jorgensen, S., and Adams, R. "Predicting Mexican-American Family Planning Intentions: An Application and Test of a Social Psychological Model." *Journal of Marriage and the Family*, Feb. 1988, *50*, 107–119.

Kalichman, S. C., and others. "Culturally Tailored HIV-AIDS Risk-Reduction Messages Targeted to African American Urban Women." *Journal of Consulting and Clinical Psychology*, 1993, *61*(2), 291–295.

Lantz, H. "Family and Kin as Revealed in the Narratives of Ex-Slaves." *Social Science Quarterly*, March 1980, *60*(4), 667–674.

Lavee, Y. "Western and Non-Western Human Sexuality: Implications for Clinical Practice." *Journal of Sex and Marital Therapy*, 1991, *17*(3), 203–213.

Lavrin, A. (ed.). *Sexuality and Marriage in Colonial Latin America*. Lincoln: University of Nebraska Press, 1989.

Lawrence, C., III. "Cringing at the Myths of Black Sexuality." In R. Chrisman and R. Allen (eds.), *Court of Appeal: The Black Community Speaks Out on the Racial and Sexual Politics of Clarence Thomas vs. Anita Hill*. New York: Ballantine, 1992.

Lister, L. (ed.). *Human Sexuality, Ethnoculture, and Social Work*. New York: Haworth Press, 1986.

McGoldrick, M., Pearce, J. K., and Giordano, J. (eds.). *Ethnicity and Family Therapy*. New York: Guilford Press, 1982.

McIntosh, E. "An Investigation of Romantic Jealousy Among Black Undergraduates." *Social Behavior and Personality*, 1989, *17*(2), 135–141.

Magana, J. R., and Carrier, J. M. "Mexican and Mexican American Male Sexual Behavior and Spread of AIDS in California." *Journal of Sex Research*, 1991, *28*(3), 425–441.

Marin, G., and Marin, B. V. "Perceived Credibility of Channels and Sources of AIDS Information Among Hispanics." *AIDS Education and Prevention*, 1990, *2*(2), 154–161.

Mays, V. M., Cochran, S. D., Bellinger, G., and Smith, R. G. "The Language of Black Gay Men's Sexual Behavior: Implications for AIDS Risk Reduction." *Journal of Sex Research*, Aug. 1992, *29*(3), 425–434.

Mindel, C. H., Habenstein, R. W., and Wright, R., Jr.(eds.). *Ethnic Families in America: Patterns and Variations*. (3rd ed.) New York: Elsevier North Holland, 1988.

Muecke, J. A. "Mother Sold Food, Daughter Sells Her Body: The Cultural Continuity of Prostitution." *Social Science and Medicine*, 1992, *35*(7), 891–901.

Newcomer, S. F., and Udry, J. R. "Oral Sex in an Adolescent Population." *Archives of Sexual Behavior*, 1985, *14*(1), 41–46.

Noh Ahn, H., and Gilbert, N. "Cultural Diversity and Sexual Abuse Prevention." *Social Service Review*, Sept. 1992, *66*(3), 410–427.

Norris, A. E., and Ford, K. "Beliefs About Condoms and Accessibility of Condoms in Hispanic and African American Youth." *Hispanic Journal of Behavioral Sciences*, 1992, *14*(3), 373–382.

Oggins, J., Leber, D., and Veroff, J. "Race and Gender Differences in Black and White Newlyweds' Perceptions of Sexual and Marital Relations." *Journal of Sex Research*, 1993, *30*(2), 152–160.

Ortiz, S., and Casas, J. M. "Birth Control and Low-Income Mexican-American Women: The Impact of Three Values." *Hispanic Journal of the Behavioral Sciences*, Feb. 1990, *12*(1), 83–92.

Ostrow, D. G., and others. "Racial Differences in Social Support and Mental Health in Men with HIV Infection: A Pilot Study." *AIDS Care*, 1991, 3(1), 55–62.

Padilla, E. R., and O'Grady, K. E. "Sexuality Among Mexican Americans: A Case of Sexual Stereotyping." *Journal of Personality and Social Psychology*, 1987, 52, 5–10.

Parker, R. G. *Bodies, Pleasures and Passions: Sexual Culture in Contemporary Brazil*. Boston: Beacon Press, 1991.

Pete, J. M., and DeSantis, L. "Sexual Decision Making in Young Black Adolescent Females." *Adolescence*, Spring 1990, 25(97), 145–154.

Price, J. H., and Miller, P. A. "Sexual Fantasies of Black and White College Students." *Psychological Reports*, 1984, 54, 1007–1014.

Priest, R. "Child Sexual Abuse Histories Among African-American College Students: A Preliminary Study." *American Journal of Orthopsychiatry*, July 1992, 62(3), 475–477.

Quinn, S. C. "AIDS and the African American Woman: The Triple Burden of Race, Class, and Gender." *Health Education Quarterly*, 1993, 20(3), 305–320.

Rao, K., and others. "Child Sexual Abuse of Asians Compared with Other Populations." *Journal of the American Academy of Child and Adolescent Psychiatry*, Sept. 1992, 31(5), 800.

Razack, S. "What Is to Be Gained by Looking White People in the Eye? Culture, Race, and Gender in Cases of Sexual Violence." *Signs: Journal of Women in Culture and Society*, 1994, 19(4), 894–923.

Rhodes, F., and Wolitski, R. J. "Perceived Effectiveness of Fear Appeals in AIDS Education: Relationship to Ethnicity, Gender, Age, and Group Membership." *AIDS Education and Prevention*, 1990, 2(1), 1–11.

St. Lawrence, J. S. "African-American Adolescents' Knowledge, Health-Related Attitudes, Sexual Behavior and Contraceptive Decisions—Implications for the Prevention of Adolescent HIV Infection." *Journal of Consulting and Clinical Psychology*, 1993, 61(1), 104–112.

Schinke, S. P., and others. "African-American and Hispanic-American Adolescents, HIV Infection, and Preventative Intervention." *AIDS Education and Prevention*, Dec. 1990, 2(4), 305–312.

Simpson, R. "The Afro-American Female: The Historical Context of the Construction of Sexual Identity." In A. Snitow, C. Stansell, and S. Thompson (eds.), *Powers of Desire: The Politics of Sexuality*. New York: Monthly Review Press, 1983.

Smith, E. A., and Udry, J. R. "Coital and Non-Coital Sexual Behaviors of White and Black Adolescents." *American Journal of Public Health*, 1985, *75*, 1200–1203.

Sorenson, S. B., and Siegel, J. M. "Gender, Ethnicity, and Sexual Assault: Findings from a Los Angeles Study." *Journal of Social Issues*, Mar. 1992, *48*(1), 93–104.

South, S., and Felson, R. "The Racial Patterning of Rape." *Social Forces*, Sept. 1990, *69*(1), 71–93.

Staples, R. *The Black Family: Essays and Studies*. (5th ed.) Belmont, Calif.: Wadsworth, 1994.

Staples, R., and Johnson, L. B. *Black Families at the Crossroads: Challenges and Prospects*. San Francisco: Jossey-Bass, 1993.

Sue, D. W., and Sue, D. *Counseling the Culturally Different: Theory and Practice*. New York: Wiley, 1992.

Suggs, D. N., and Miracle, A. W. (eds.). *Culture and Human Sexuality*. Belmont, Calif.: Wadsworth, 1993.

Sullivan, C. "Pathways to Infection: AIDS Vulnerability Among the Navajo." *AIDS Education and Prevention*, 1991, *3*(3), 241–257.

Takaki, R. *From Different Shores: Perspectives on Race and Ethnicity in America*. New York: Oxford University Press, 1994.

Thomas, S. B., and Quinn, S. C. "The Tuskegee Syphilis Study, 1932 to 1972: Implications for HIV Education and AIDS Risk Education Programs in the Black Community." *American Journal of Public Health*, Nov. 1991, *81*(11), 1498–1504.

Thompson, V.L.S., and West, S. D. "Attitudes of African American Adults Toward Treatment in Cases of Rape." *Community Mental Health Journal*, 1992, *28*(6), 546–561.

Thornton, A., and Camburn, D. "The Influence of the Family on Premarital Sexual Attitudes and Behavior." *Demography*, Aug. 1987, *24*(3), 323–340.

Timberlake, C., and Carpenter, W. D. "Sexuality Attitudes of Black Adults." *Family Relations*, 1990, *39*, 87–91.

Torres, A., and Singh, S. "Contraceptive Practice Among Hispanic Adolescents." *Family Planning Perspectives*, July 1986, *18*(4), 193–194.

Tucker, M. B., and Taylor, R. J. "Demographic Correlates of Relationship Status Among Black Americans." *Journal of Marriage and the Family*, 1989, *51*, 655–665.

Vasquez-Nuthall, E., and others. "Sex Roles and Perceptions of Femininity and Masculinity of Hispanic Women: A Review of the Literature." *Psychology of Women Quarterly*, 1987, *11*, 409–426.

Wyatt, G. E. "Examining Ethnicity Versus Race in AIDS-Related Sex Research." *Social Science and Medicine*, 1991, *33*(1), 37–45.

Wyatt, G. E., and Lyons-Rowe, S. "African American Women's Sexual Satisfaction as a Dimension of Their Sex Roles." *Sex Roles*, Apr. 1990, *22*(7–8), 509–524.

Zinn, M. Baca, "Chicano Men and Masculinity," *The Journal of Ethnic Studies*, *10*(2), 29–44.

Index